forwardpoetry

LIFE'S PRISM

A COLLECTION OF POETRY

EDITED BY JENNI BANNISTER

forwardpoetry

First published in Great Britain in 2015 by:
Forward Poetry
Remus House
Coltsfoot Drive
Peterborough
PE2 9BF

Telephone: 01733 890099
Website: www.forwardpoetry.co.uk

SB ISBN 978-1-84418-692-1

Printed and bound in the UK by BookPrintingUK
Website: www.bookprintinguk.com

FOREWORD

Here at Forward Poetry our aim has always been to provide a bridge to publication for unknown poets and allow their work to reach a wider audience. We believe that poetry should not be exclusive or elitist but available to be accessed and appreciated by all.

We hope you will agree that our latest collection with its combination of traditional and modern verse is one that everyone can enjoy. Whether you prefer humorous rhymes or poignant odes there is something inside these pages that will suit every reader's taste.

We are very proud to present this anthology and we are sure it will provide entertainment and inspiration for years to come.

CONTENTS

forwardpoetry

THE POEMS

MY TIME

Is there time to live in full
Is there time to be you
It's my time to spend

When is time worth spending
Can time be too short
Should we waste it anyhow

Most of time is here then gone
Why be scared when it's done
I've used it how I wanted

My time is full of surprises
Tears, smiles, happiness
Sadness and pain

For the rest of time
However long it may be
Once it's gone it's gone.

KEVIN JACKSON

Unfit Me (Teeheehee)

Opened my closet and got a shock
Filled to the brim with seventies stock
Tried things on but they didn't fit
Held my belly in but they still split

Whatever happened to my slender figure
When I say I was thin, the peeps, they snigger
Gotta get off this great big ass
Get out walking and rid of this gas!

Have to get out there on the road
Away from the line I've always toed
I do know how to talk the talk
But now it's time to walk the walk

Up and down the road I'll go
Well down anyways, but up, hell no!
Instead of lifts the stairs I'll climb
Soon I'll be taking them two at a time

The peeps that laughed at unfit me
Will laugh at me no more, you'll see
I'm gonna be a babe, I'll be 'all that'
I'll even get rid of my seventies tat

Walking the dog I'll be so cool
No puffin' and pantin' that's the rule
So give me time, a year or more
And I'll be a very fit me for sure

Now that I've finished this little rhyme
I'll go to sleep 'cos it's bedtime
Up in the morning early and bright
Noo! That does not sound right

Oh darn it all, I'll make some tea
Have a chocolate biscuit or three
Now snuggled up on the settee
With my biscuits and my tea
I'm thinking of the morning with no glee
Don't think this exercise thing's for me!

Anne Craig

Behind A Veil Of Silence

Engulfed as I ponder in a decadent gaze,
fixation on her radiant, malevolent ways.
How thoughtless that these memories cling with no remorse,
oh, how I beg them to fade.
Retaining commendments to be held so dear
you gesture our bonds, intentions so clear.
Upon first glance, a mere common leering,
behind sweet fickle eyes, untampered concealing.
Laced in black satin, only to hide what would lie beneath.
Still hidden, kept oblivious to those of affection,
to incarcerate oneself, such bewildered selection.
How quickly I was scorned and sunk by such perverse jealousy.
Those endless legs scarred from a previous bonding
'Who hurt you?' I utter, as I course through your tresses, consoling I stroke,
but beneath would lie a mutual lust between us now broke.
My darling, I'm only too happy to oblige.
Coerced through our ravenous, twisted arrays
to a verbal allure, displaced in our ways.
So eclipsing was this waste of space that some may call a heart,
her embrace would linger on, forbidden to depart.
You never held me so tight . . .
Erased, internally I bellow, begging reconciliation,
unchained I bare the ruptured force, blessed divination.
A blistering elation, forced reclamation all would see,
alas, unbound emptiness, my eventuality.
Beckoned by her heart, if only forcefully misled,
vaster floods of crimson wine undoubtedly be shed.
If only just to see your eyes again . . .
Heart striking she shines, embracing decline,
still she hides, behind a veil of silence.

Steven Kuhn

Still Yet Ourselves

(Sidhe – ***Shee, Spirit)***

The Long Night has come and gone
Our Long Dark has ended with candles dawn
Light of Winter, candles Sidhe shining bright
Stars burning against fears, all ignorances Night
Still yet ourselves
Against the beacon of love's memories
The tides of centuries darkness beat in vain . . .

Still yet ourselves

Despite stupid teachers
Despite obtuse preachers
Still yet ourselves
One spirit, mind and heart
Sword and shields, compassions, strength
Still yet ourselves surprised by yourselves
Our children
Each glimpse a sip of revelation
Consummation of spirit joy
Still yet ourselves astonished by yourselves
Such passion, such dreams
Such vision, such assuredness
Still yet ourselves, beguiled by yourselves
Our victory, our justice
Our love, our pride
Our future
Still yet ourselves, yourselves
So much more than ourselves.

John Graham

DARK EYES

Out of the mist a spirit
An angel with dark eyes
He hypnotised her soul
She was took in by his lies
He held her heart in his hands
Filled her with desire
Pulled her body close to his
Her insides set on fire

Her legs grew weak
She lost all sense
His lips pressed into hers
Her innocence she gave freely
As heaven inside stirred

With the deepest cut
He carved her heart
Heaven turned to hell
The devil in disguise revealed
As morning daylight fell.

SUSAN WORRALL

Put Your Hope In Me

As you sit and ponder and find that you have no hope,
then look up and place your hope in Him.

I remember rejoicing with the angels
as I watched you being created.
Long before you were ever a thought
in your parents' minds
I had laid out a plan for your life.
When I crooned over you inside your
mother's womb, it was Me who sang the
soft lullaby of promising you then, that I
would always be with you.

My Dearest Child, I long so much for you
to turn to me and place your heart in my hand.
I have such blessings in store for you, that all Heaven waits
in anticipation for you to receive them.
Yet I cannot force them upon you my Child.
You must reach out and trust in Me
and I will never let you down.
When hope has left you and you are all alone,
that is when my Hope will touch you and set you free.

What is your Hope Lord, I hear you ask
That differs so much from mine?
Ah, the difference is my Child, My Hope lies
within you waiting for the time
that He can spring up and lift you beyond all understanding.
Then my Hope will set you free once again, to hear my voice,
to lift your eyes and see beyond the darkness that surrounds you.
Then you will come to Me and I will sing once
more again the lullaby of old.
That I will always be with you no matter
what the future holds.

Come my Child you are the apple of my eye.
I dance and sing over you.
Come my Child and trust in Me
and walk in the plans I have for thee . . .

Elizabeth Jane Bastow

ALICE OF OZ

She walks along the street
Down the yellow brick road
Alice beaming like a Cheshire Cat
Trying to find her way back home
Her smile like a hurricane
Causing destruction to whomever she meets
A femme fatale in dream worlds
Film noir paradise for every man
The gun slowly lifting to his head
Only for liquor to make him sober
Her beauty like an iron fist
Conquering oceans with one swoop
He leans against an automobile
Takes a swipe of his cigarette
Smiles back
A gun shot
Birds head south for the winter
She as lonely as him
They never meet
Only in movies.

GEORGE SIVETIDIS

Beneath The Waves

'Can you hear me?' she screamed,
Her voice rippling across the upturned sea,
Vibrations shook the ground a-split,
But they could not awaken love in me.

Her crimson nails tore at my prune-like skin,
Their watery scrapes denoted futility,
For it was not my life that ebbed away,
It was my heart that had been lost at sea.

The rhythmic thud, the layering beat,
Smashed off my metallic coating,
The tin man in all his glory,
Content in this immersive floating.

Her dewy eyes were wild,
Her oval mouth frozen in dizzying dread,
But I drifted peacefully in sunshine's calm,
All in all, quite brain dead.

Sarah-Jane Coyle

My Darling Nanny Mary

My darling Nanny Mary
Our hearts are breaking today,
As heaven requested your presence – with us you can no longer stay.
You made our lives so happy, gave your love wherever you were -
it breaks my heart to know you'll no longer be where we are.
Every day you've been there whenever we've needed a friend,
even when our constant noise has driven you round the bend.
We've shared so many things together, the list goes on and on -
My favourite being you getting to know my boys, your precious great grandsons.
Everyone of us adored you
You filled our hearts with glee
Now that you are gone Nanny,
please watch over me.

Lynsey Draper

Walk Away

It's the feeling when waking at 3am
Thinking of you and me back when
Our words would last right into the night
When you'd go to bed in the morning light
Back when things were easy and clear
I was never going to lose you, my dear
I thought our future was bright and bold
I never listened to what I was told
I saw the signs and the complications
The misused words and the same frustrations
I pushed them all away from my mind
Trying to believe that all was fine
Now all you seem to do is leave
It's becoming harder for me to breathe
This connection is crumbling in my hand
Slipping through my fingers like grains of sand
And it hurts when you're here and it hurts when you're gone
And the minutes get shorter until there are none
It was never meant to feel this way
And it's getting harder every day
You tell me these words that I know you don't mean
How could I ever believe in this dream?
You have no idea how much this is hurting
Whenever I'm sleeping or crying or working
You'll be somewhere doing whatever you love
While I will be telling myself to give up
I send you these messages all of the time
You never send me one back or even reply
And maybe you think I'm strong and unbroken
While I'm still insecure and wishing and hoping
Because I'm giving you everything that I have
Yet it feels like you're giving me nothing back
For hours and hours I'm waiting for you
And thinking of us is all that I do
And I wonder if I even cross your mind
When you're doing something else all of the time

I'm a substitute girl until you find someone else
Who can please you and be there and make your heart melt

And that's how I knew we were already ending
Long before your answer was pending
So go find your princess and know I'll be fine
All I'll need is a little time.

GEORGIA HEAD

I Am Not Sure Why It Walks My Mind

I am not sure why it walks my mind

But I have never felt so undeserving as now
I have never been as godless
We lie in the hours aching for change as it interrupts us like an honest dawn.

To bear the burden of wasted efforts is finalising
Not for me the prophetic ramblings or rough edged revolutionary

What will I do after the final hours of love and guidance

After the dinners and the mornings
After that slow cooked and lingering smell
And after those long and those wind beaten walks.

I once walked out onto the deck and watched birds ascending to sun

I am a youth so keenly aware of my own fragility.

Eleanor Perry

Isaac

(There was no other before me
and there would be no other after.)

The eyes of a ward or clinic
continue to fixate on my father,
John,
a nervous sculpture in the absence
of his woman's screams.

(He always did bite his nails.)

I was taken to the delivery room;
the temple mount,
where mother and I lie,
silent in unconscious anticipation
of the things to come.
The sparse bed, the hospital-altar braces
itself as I am sliced out,
Isaac,
unbound by a masked angel in
bloodied garb.

But I am rushed, rushed to an empty
incubator, chair of Elijah, my father following
a disciple, gives consent
and I am cut in covenant
eight days too early.

Upon passing into their arms,
both my fathers weep.

BRENDAN PHILIP BRADY

Children

Children may be annoying,
Children may be irritating,
Yes, this may be true,
But there is no one like you.

You've been there through my toughest times,
Through the thickest and thinnest,
Brightest and dimmest.

Your laughter and childish sounds,
Make me so proud,
Those times I can call you
My greatest friend.

Young people are vulnerable,
Young people are noisy,
Young people may act hard
But underneath all that,
They are still children.

Holly G Wilson

Soldier In All Of Us

There is a soldier in all of us, each of the soldiers has his
own battles within life.
Each of those battles can be won
or lost and with each victory the soldier gets more
confident.
But with each defeat the soldier becomes
stronger and more prepared for the battles to come.

Sometimes the soldier may have to face an army
through the battle,
even though there may be no hope
of victory the soldier will stand by us and fight for us.

Even if defeat stares at us in a losing battle the soldier
never gives up.
As time passes the solider within us gets
wiser and more powerful,
so the soldier can be stronger
when we are defeated.

The lost battles are lost in valour
and honour.
Sometimes we feel that we have lost the
soldier within us from the fought battle.
That feeling may stick there for a long time but in the
end the soldier always comes back to fight for us
another day or life.

As the soldier within us gets to the
end of his time the soldier feels more peaceful,
as there
are no more battles that need to be fought that are
worth fighting.

Then at once the soldier can be admired
in peace with no battles to fight,
no more defeats to be
had till the end of his days.

MICHAL NIEDZIELSKI

Knowledge

London is the capital of the world,
With some places and streets that I've never heard,
Driving along every day on my bike,
Looking around at whatever I like,
The cold mornings aren't so bad,
But it's the pouring rain that drives you mad,
The black cab drivers look at me with regret,
Knowing they were here too, which they want to just forget,
Balls to it all, I say each evening,
Why should I do it, what am I learning,
Dole money, that's a joke,
You can give it to another bloke,
Well it's goodbye for now, I say that with very much disdain,
For I'm getting out this knowledge lark, it's driving me bloody insane.

Philip Rugg

THE GUIDING LIGHT

Search yourself so deep
Find your soul with all your might
And you will find eternal love
Then you will find your guiding light

It was sent from Heaven
And it will truly be yours
And it can open
So many doors

Use it wisely
For your destiny
And it will guide you
It's so Heavenly

The light will shine
Follow its track
Where love will hold
So don't hold back

Cos once you have found it
You will wake one fine day
Now that you will know
You will be truly on your way.

DARREN BLY

I Don't Want To Be Alone

I want to talk to you, down the phone
I don't want to be alone
I want to tell you how I feel
Love may never blossom, but friendships last forever
I just want you to be there
I just want someone to care
Someone to be around, someone to just listen
I cannot see where this is going, love and friendships are rare
I just want to hear your voice, I just want to know you care
And if you care just a little
You will be happy to listen
To me down the phone
In times of need, I don't want to be alone
Just listen to my voice
Learn about my hopes and dreams
Listen to my downfalls
A voice of reason, an ear to listen
A heart that cares
Thank you for being there.

Greg Foley

BIPOLAR

He has her by the throat.
Suffocated of speech, she screams inside,
His immobilising hands explore her fears.

Desperate to break free, writhing in misery, she waits.
She will be happy again.

Choking on her loneliness she cries,
Her desperation for human contact burns her skin, but she can't escape.
He has her by the throat.

He's always there.
He whispers to her, until the words embed into her mind like maggots
'Why are you alive?'

Tearing, scratching, pulling, ripping
There is no escape,
He has her by the throat.

She sees the sunrise,
Feels the warmth against her skin,
His grip loosens.

Her laugh dances in the wind,
She is free.

Maybe one day he won't come back.

ISABEL HUDSON

If I Could!

Should I follow sunlight through a prism
After, my imagination's been led
I would step on a rainbow's colours,
From violet to red
I'd blow away air pollution, that makes
The skies seem white
There would be a clean sky, a blue sky
And our future would seem bright.

Peter Hickman

HELP ME TO START AGAIN

In a pool of pain and bitterness,
Comforted by contrition and unexplainable love,
I looked into the skies with my hands high . . .
I closed my naked eyes and asked why.

I have been here before . . . I'm here again,
Same gathering in the same demented atmosphere.
A kind-hearted dove that mingles with the cassowaries . . .
A familiar start with a predicted end.

Why did I flee from you O Lord?
Why is this path so cold O Lord?
My father prayed . . . my mother wept!
Help me O Lord to start again!

Now I claim that pain is hope
As sunrise is far and its light so faint.
Once played a saint but now a villain
As the story is told again and again.

As his wrinkle strengthens and brags,
As her fine black hair turns grey,
The flesh still in the gathering and did not understand . . .
The spirit looks down and shakes his head.

NDIDI UBOGU

Departure

Whether rags to riches.
Rich or poor . . .
The only thing I'm taking to the grave
Is the will to live

Imagine all of life's riddles finally solved.
Imagine not getting old.
Let the truth be told.
A slave to God
But I'm never getting sold.
I still got my soul.
I've still even got goals.
I'm still with you in spirit.
And now I must go.

Aaron Joseph Henry Noel

The Purple Sun

The purple sun that rises in the west,
Why do I feel like my day has just begun,
When it's reached the finish?

The purple sun that orbits the Earth,
Why do I feel like anybody cares,
When I'm the only one who does?

The purple sun that burns darker than yesterday,
Why do I feel like I'm getting wiser,
When it's just illusion, clouding my judgement?

The purple sun that shines over
The grey rainbows and
The green of the street
That keeps the world standing still.

Why do I feel like I'm getting any richer, when the purple sun blisters my cash?
Because that's what keeps the world standing still.

That's what keeps the world standing still.

Curtis Stearn

Blind Girl

We two had a week,
Love was at it's peak.
Things we did, things said,
Sat upon my bed.
For this I confess,
My deepest desire.
My hope to impress,
My love on a spire.

We two had a week,
Words I dare not speak,
Uttered from my mind,
Lost to the world, blind.
But woe,
And pain,
Doth flow,
And stain.

We two had a week,
Thought I was a freak,
The things I said, dumb,
Our hearts, heads, dead, numb.
But love is gone,
From my heart,
There just is none,
I can't start.

We two had a week,
Me, a love struck geek.
My heart desolate,
My soul, deficit.
Please go, leave me now,
Walk on, through a door.
Lift of hat, a bow,
or wait, what's in store?

Jacob Benjamin

House Of Pages

I used to build my own house of pages
construct rhythm and rhyme on my fingertips
now I'm a victim of regular structure and phrases
with not a single word I like on my lips.

I used to view this as a need
word for word came as a relief
now I have nothing else to talk about
I'm in a house of pages and can't write myself out.

Karolina Tauer

The Uncertain Man

Sing songs and watch the flowers fall
over your brow, upon your nose.
Entwined stem to stem
craft, from a people of old.

You shake it back
with hands by your side
shaking your head, back and forwards
to the sound of sonorous laughter
from you, and the others.

Clothes of cloth
white as clouds
on this sunny day
drape over your figure
like a willow on the lake
and flutters like a feather
in a playful breeze.

As you dance round the maypole
with ribbon in one palm
trailing hand in hand
to form a circle
of unbridled joy, innocence.

Not aware that one was there
staring through astonishment
where cynicism couldn't bear.
Hoping not to be noticed
though longing for the attention
the eyes, the pupils, the face
to know I stood, stared and breathed.

A beggar, a mortal, an urchin
among the pure.
Pure as
flesh and blood could be.
Noise was to be made
that was certain, that was sure.
Either I, in form of greeting
or from them in the form of a shout
A scream, a gasp, a wretch at the obscene.

I hold my words, my breath
and my anonymity
I am only human

though less in my mind
I dream in idealism
and live in envy
In the shadows to the side.

When I could no longer bear it
I turn, I sigh
and linger
then start to tread the muddy path
back to mine.
Away from the beat and track
angel songs and daisy chains.

To the place I reside
On the periphery of your eye
Out of people's attention
back to the place I hide.
Where the only company is my dog
my demons and my silhouette
cast across the room
large, black and bare.

Exactly where you are not.

MATTHEW PHILLIPS

A Question Of Purity

Cherry blossoms float to the dark open floor,
their petals dire and weak.
Curtains of the sky close around the contaminated earth
and the religious gather in the awaiting pews.
Oh how their choruses fill the solemn air,
pouring their perfect truth upon our weary, worldly carcasses.
I am drawn along by the Pied Piper's flute like a blind rat,
lined in an assembly of bitter truth.
Our tongues pulled by the puppeteer,
we are merely puppets held by societal strings,
made to dance and swing
to the hymns.
We are no longer bound to the chains that kept us captive
they preach
No, we are now bounded by locks that only ***their*** tongues can unlock.
Wistfully we eat the thoughts they feed into the matter beneath our skull.
Penetrating our thoughts, desires and dreams,
we fall victim to a religious choreographed performance.
The theatrics tame our empty pockets,
pushing us deeper into the wooden seats.
Testimonial script melted the love of Tammuz and Ishtar, sculpted by the hands of a maternal womb.
We are birthed into a dystopian world view,
our umbilical cords connected to the placenta of blindness.
Everyone attached, to the same rhythm
a sea of clones murdering individuality,
Let the tears along our faces rejoice to the birth of a religious normality.
The songs of countless sinners ferment from below,
Rotten corpses and tired, closed eyes,
All alike beneath their gravestones.
Dust returning to dust.
Dirt upon dirt.
If only they could hear the whispers of our moans,
And exclaim in the light of the full moon,
there is no difference between you and I.
Winter is coming soon,
the rotten leaves fall to the ground.
Let the bitter frost calm the tremble of my bones.
A deep fear rooted, planted and de-seeded
I march along the yellow brick road, the flute placed firmly in my hands.
Watch them come in their masses, I think inside.
The Pied Piper and I, singing the same old melody.

His lips drip rehearsed words, my head nods in agreement with the crowd.
Clap, clap, clap, clap, clap,
From the depths of the dirt, trees grow and sing,
Oh what a day it is, that you shall become a duplicate in a religious reproduction.
A born sinner, seeking an unfound perfection.
Their eyes blank and dull, not a whisper do they utter from their transgressed tongues.
Their thighs pray to the tune, as their hips part like the red sea, swaying side to side.
They lift their hands in unison, clapping the drum,
Take a bow they say, the theatrics is done.
The prayers of countless sinners ferment from below,
Rotten corpses and tired, closed eyes,
All alike beneath their gravestones.
Dust returning to dust.
Dirt upon dirt.
If only they could hear the whispers of our moans,
And exclaim in the light of the full moon,
There is no difference between you and I.
Summer is coming soon.
The heat of a glistened moon, soaks into the pores of the sinking sun.
The melody of the flute floats to my ears, swaying my hips,
to the beat of an unfriendly tune.
No longer seeking a perfection, my flesh cannot perceive,
the doors bolted shut, backs turned from my wistful look.
I am a sinner they say, to impure to be made pure in a place meant to abolish impurity.
I am baptised in the waters of judgement,
And resurrected like Osiris.
Oh! Let the feathers of dust, moulded against my god given flesh
cry out at this earthly
abandonment.
As the falling dove tears the white sky in two,
stares bare into my Egyptian brown skin.
Stitch my limbs back together ***my love***, I cannot withstand such disdain.
Not even the Pied Piper's flute rings from within.
The tears of countless sinners ferment from below,
Rotten corpses and tired, closed eyes,
All alike beneath their gravestones.
Dust returning to dust.
Dirt upon dirt.
If only they could hear the echoes of our moans,
And exclaim in the light of the full moon,
There is no difference between you and I.
The Pied Piper's song is now silent.
All around me, people gather like rats and point far from the forbidden distance of Eden.
Tears surrender my faith, falling upon my birth-given desires.
They say I am religiously too impure to call upon the lord,

My attraction to Bathsheba, they say, is a moulded tomb inside my clitoris,
Deporting me towards the showers of Hades.
I am now the city of Atlantis, buried six feet deep in the battle of humanity,
I love her, my bones whisper
As condemnation buries my prayers.
Let this Odyssey of a trip not quieten my dragon tongue.
I am, I am, I am,
A product of stars.
A purity of so-called impurity,
A unique specimen of a diamond reflecting the universe.
I am awakened by my unseen conscious mind, I am no different to ***you***,
And you are no different to ***I***.
My rainbow heart, reflects upon your blue sky thoughts.
Let the religious impurity be laid to rest,
As ashes turn to ashes,
And dust into dust.
Let the Pied Piper's flute be silenced at ***once***.

SIMONE D JAMES

How I Feel

From heaven you came and blew my mind
You left me breathless, you left me mindless
Without you I find it hard to breathe
Without you my heart stops to beat
I am all alone like a body without a soul
So I shall not run, I shall not hide, soon our paths will collide
We must face each other and deal with our plight
I see you like no one else does
What is mine has become yours
Together we can remove any hurdles
For that I must clear my mind and listen to my heart
Let me hear what I want, and then we will never be apart.

Suki Kaur Dhaliwal

I Stand

I stand, surrounded, on the brink of an endless ocean,
In an empty world, of a thousand wonders.
Gaelic echoes, through a people born to speak it,
Water like blood, flows through an island's veins.

I stand, lost, in the shadow of the tallest mountain,
In this heart-stealing land, of everlasting beauty.
Each single track road, weaves its place through time,
A world, through a viewfinder, stained in amber gold.

I stand, in awe, as nature dictates the calm before the storm,
At the foot of a village, carved into the hillside.
A chilling wind, cuts through each forgotten blackhouse,
The defeated sun, lies through a clouded sky.

Jacob Hesmondhalgh

FOUND I LATER RHYMED (BALLADE)

I was lost in the sadness of a shadow,
dampening the dream of a happy soul.
It followed from behind like a dark cloak.
Did not see it coming, as I recall,
catching up when I was starting to fall.
Looking at the light, shadow was behind;
silently lurking, hoping I would stall.
Shaded sadness faded when I later rhymed.

Seasoning thoughts, to make sentences flow,
sent this dark shadow down to Hades Hall.
Climbed from the pit, which gripped feet from below;
stopped shuddering sadness win a frightful crawl.
A bright sun shone when I at last stood tall.
Words of wisdom were like a gold dust find;
mined from minds of poets were verses galore.
Shaded sadness faded when I later rhymed.

I once thought my shadow would never go,
when a decade ago its shade had a ball,
but, sadness was sorry to suffer this blow.
Just like a fisherman, with a large trawl,
I found contentment, words being my haul.
Lines of rhyme seemed like fish of a kind,
carefully selected was fit for all.
Shaded sadness faded when I later rhymed.

I could not sense shadow behind me at all,
but I could let in light, open the blind.
Disperse the gloom. Dapple-shade install.
Shaded sadness faded when I later rhymed.

PHILIP H SIMMONS

Missing.

Gone, from the sandpit,
Nana's garden, home.
Leaving behind a cap,
A shoe, a phone.
Struggling or fed
Candy promises
They roam.

Gone, from the playground,
The day care, the street.
Unnoticed the absence
Of tiny little feet.
Parents unaware of the
Monsters they meet.

Gone, from the school gates,
The buggy, their bed.
Searching for any sign
Of one little head.
After a while when the
Beasts have fled.

Gone. In a nettle ditch,
A bin, a car.
After they're done
They don't go far.
The little bodies leave
A permanent scar.

Gone from the sandpit,
Nana's garden, home.

Emily Court

The Snowflake

With the hellish whistles blowing, hold a dying comrade's hand
While his life-blood slowly trickles through the sacking to the sand
of these bags that mark a border where we're told to stand and kill
For the bureaucrats and rich men far behind us, living still.
So we face the daily torment of the shooting and the shell
of this god-forsaken border that's become a living hell
and we take it and we take it but the generals never cared
they just say that they will shoot us if we run because we're scared.
Just a soldier who was sent here, now it's time to do or die
try to choke back the emotion as they say men shouldn't cry
So I watch a single snowflake fall upon my comrade's chest
soaking up some blood that lays there as it turns from white to red
turns the colour of the poppy that will grow here in the spring
and I wonder if I'll see them when the seasons turn again.

Christmas Eve and snow has fallen on the mud and blood and sand
of the bags that line our trenches on the edge of no-man's-land
If I came into your trenches would you shoot me on first sight
or extend a hand through darkness with a Christmas wish this night?

Simon Hackney

Dining With The Devil

There was a side of you that I have always ignored
You have always showed me your brightest side
When you saved me from falling apart
I have always been comforted with your smile
I thought I knew the best of you
Because you taught me how to love you
I thought I knew you more than anybody
But in fact you were wearing a disguise
Today I am facing the truth
That you are not as good as you did pretend
And tonight I am having dinner with the Devil
The Devil that you are and that only today I really discovered.

Sitting around the table with you
Watching you sipping that red wine
Makes me faint and weak
I need to run away from your claws
Because I don't want to be your prey
But where should I go?
Where could I go?
There is nowhere I could feel safe
Outside your comfort zone
Even though I now know who you really are
The taste of your presence around me
Is kind of bittersweet and dangerous
But today I am facing the truth
That you are not as good as you did pretend
And tonight I am having dinner with the Devil
The Devil that you are and that only today I really discovered.

I am trembling from head to toes
Because the truth is scaring me
And I surrender my life to the Devil that you are
I see the flames coming out from your hands
As you are trying to touch me
And telling me that I shouldn't be so shaky
You embraced me and pull my head to your heart
And when you did it I felt your heartbeat

This made me realise that you were crying
I never knew that even a devil could cry
And as you were walking me to the table
You whispered that all you want from me
Is to stay one more time with you
And dine with you for the last time.

MICHELLE NOUNGA

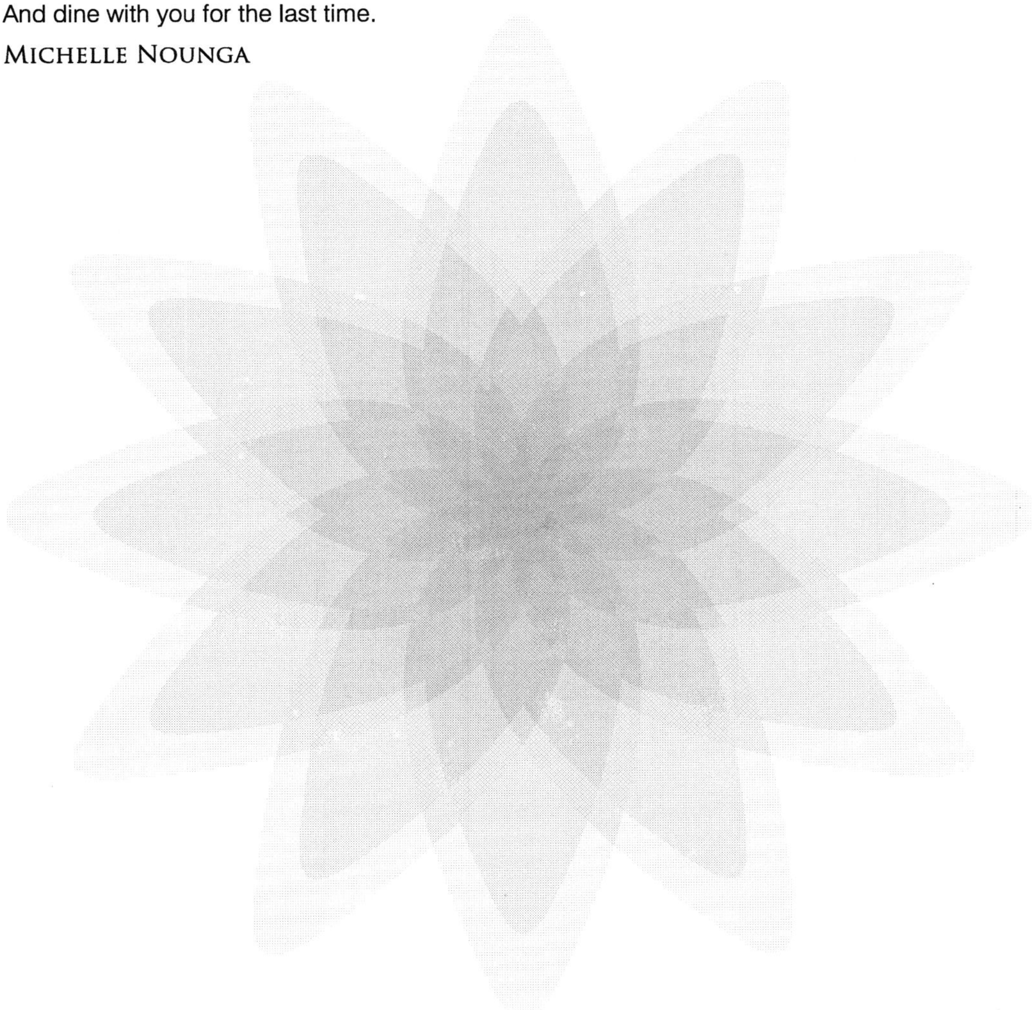

Love's Eternity

For you to me are everything
From me to you this letter I bring
I give you my body, I give you my mind
I give you my heart 'til the end of time

For you are my girl who is now part of me
My love for you burns for eternity
I give my courage, I give you my strength
I give you my passion from Heaven's scent

When I sleep at night I dream of you
Under the stars looking at the moon
My spirit travels through the night
So I can be right by your side

As my warm breath caresses your lips
Our bodies entwine, forever we kiss
As we move closer we become one
Our life together has now just begun.

James Coupland

THE DESTRUCTION OF POMPEII

Earth trembled, ground shook,
Skies became grey.
When I woke up this morning,
It was just a normal day.

Burning on the mountain,
At the very top.
Pressure built up,
Then rocks started to drop.

A dense black cloud,
Overflowing with ash
Blocked out the light
And came down with a crash.

There's ash and rocks,
Floating in the sky.
I don't know the cause,
I don't understand why.

Crowds of screaming people,
All fleeing in terror.
'Something must have gone wrong,
There must be an error.'

This unexpected explosion
Caused terror and fright.
The ash kept on falling,
All day and all night.

The eruption destroyed
Many homes and scenery.
Everything was grey,
There was no more greenery.

Earth trembled, ground shook,
Skies became grey.
When I woke up this morning,
It was just a normal day.

EMILY JESSOP

The Prison Library

No mobile phones
But cellular voices pervade this graceful place
Carefully caressed curses and echoes into its wooden shelves
Heated chatter burns down to choral embers
Slightly quieter than the Waterloo and City line
Bio's bibles and suicide notes secrete from this otherwise
Civilised revision of a literary den
Those playing chess mutter cultured observations of their time at Her Majesty's pleasure
Whilst aisles are swanned by those seeking profundity in the unknown
Orderlies rescue the dyslexic brave, the adventurous and the broken-hearted
I loiter and footle with Peter the political journalist
Positing myriad ways to occupy two and a half years
Give or take His Honour's subtractions
Magazine skimmers brace brazenly the latest quarterlies
For bums and bras
Still waters lap lazily against the disordered shores of the self-help section
Multi-faceted rough diamonds shine their prisms of light through Rosetta Stones
Beggars, burglars and banqueters steal space and time
Against a deadline of ninety minutes
Socially elastic, eclectic and often enthusiastic crowds fall in awkwardly upon each other
For support, wisdom and a skinny burn
But above all. This non revenue reading venue
Where information its greatest commodity
Freely given and widely accepted
By terrorists and freedom fighters alike
Contains revolution within its nefarious walls of dangerously free thought
Bringing hope to many, joy to few and knowledge to all
Is a sanctuary bound within barbed razor wire
Surrounded by steep grey walls where hope may die
But those who seek asylum within its creative womb
Are reborn. Quietly. Anonymously
Where manslaughter subsides revealing sensitive prose of truth
Where courage wrestles uncertainty and prevails
We find solace here
Where late fines are kindly waived for the noble and the bold
Here we of so much faith take refuge in the heightened security
Of life in the bus lane
And find comfort here where demons leave their issues at the door
And let us have our moment
Where the un-enlightened hope to embrace new states of mind
And dead presidents whisper, 'Quiet please'
Here where patience died

And softly spoken words were drowned out by harsh digs, movement and raised voices
We experience number fifty on the bucket list
And although afraid of death
These passengers are not afraid of life
And here we clamour and search
Amongst science and nature. Fact and fiction
For our own 'Piper at the gates of dawn'
And safety at the hearth of like minds
A place amongst the throes and vices of the subtle riot
To call our own.

PAUL BAICHOO

Do You Now Understand?

I wish I could understand myself
I know it's not me, it's my health
But I guess you don't see it that way
People are just ignorant and leave me astray

I dream all day and fear the night
For when my chest becomes tight
I lay on my pillow with a trail of tears
And to block out reality, I cover my ears

The sadness inside is screaming to come out
Can you not see this in my eyes when I'm about?
I know I hide all this but it's not my decision
It feels as if I have an invisible incision

I need help before it's too late
I don't remember the last time I ate
What you don't get is that it terrifies me
But I'm going to get through this, you will see

Do you now understand what it's like to have depression?
Believe me, if you hide it, there's never any progression.

Rebecca Wiltsher

UNTITLED

I have come here in the hope of finding you
Brought by chance, our flames, distinguished in the night
And fanned by disapproval, form a single fire
Our love is right, as only innocence can be
To flicker as the wind wills us; illuminating
If one of us were lost, so with this light is found

And with you there is peace
We are the centre of a storm whose passion leaves us free
And through the dark till dawn, when you will stay with me
Our love is our release.

STEVE MURRAY

The Summer Wind

The summer wind caressed her hair
as it came, blowing in from the sea -
. . . we walked, hand in hand along
the golden sand . . . my love – and me.
The summer wind kissed her face . . .
a brief embrace – then moving on in its
race . . . we knew not where – the summer
wind . . . we did not care.
The sea, placid, danced its way to
the shore . . . the tide came in, slow but
sure . . . pushed along by the summer wind.
Crusoe like footprints lay ahead -
by whom and where . . . no idea or
where they led so, we followed to the
sheltered cove, where men and women
removed their clothes to enjoy the sun
and, we would peep . . . it was just in fun.
We retraced our steps along the shore
. . . I could have stayed on my own-peeped
some more but, my love said I had seen
enough . . . much better at home! I agreed -
- my love was right so, let's go . . .don't
wait till night!
The summer wind heard our laugh -
wrapped itself around us, like a scarf . . .
warm, comforting . . . then moved on to
become, perhaps, somewhere an unwanted
draught whilst we, my girl and I, in love,
hand in hand, walked along that golden
sand . . . there was the water . . . we both
jumped in . . . but, did not swim . . . .
The summer wind caressed her hair as
it came, blowing in over the sea . . . we
walked, hand in hand along the golden

sand . . . my love – and me – so happily!
'Memories of Slapton Sands . . .
. . . the summer wind . . .
the summer wind . . .
In the summer wind'.

NORMAN LEWIS

Our Sister's Baby

When she heard your news, she didn't know what to say.
She felt your heart scream in a clasp in her chest.

When he heard your news, he threw his soul into the fire.
He pulled his hair out in the ringing of your name as her heart screamed with yours.

When the world heard your news, it was unaffected at first,
Its stony heart didn't quite break. But it pretended it did.

When they hear your news now, they well up an ocean of tears.
Guilty, salty tears that are naked, bald and burnt.

When she hears your news now, she sits through the sunset.
The birds are the little bits of your baby.

When the angels hear your news, they smile with pity.
They wonder where your heart was when you said goodbye.

When the sky hears your news, it flinches at your pain.
The world tends to look up and spit flames when it is spewing.

When she hears her news, she looks on with agonising nurture,
Everything small and silent is her baby.

When she heard your news, she fell into webs of limbs,
Sanity got tangled up in moral values.

When the baby heard your news, its unformed lips puckered,
Its little fingers uncurled into maggots ready to be cast as bait.

When the baby finally let go, it was cast out so quickly,
You didn't know that wingless creature took flight with a piece of you.

Rachel Bunn

Arrogant Love

From underneath the seas,
I stretch my mighty hands,
to surge two suffocated islands,
and design a nation that obeys.

I pen my Bible with silence,
to command the sunrise,
split the seas in two,
as I march to lands,

No man dares to say,
where I shall stay,
They all read my Bible,
Even the illiterate of them,

Worship my idols,
Submit to my conducts,
or abandon,
for whichever you choose,
I wrote your fate already.

In the obscurity of my prisons,
I'll throw you,
In the burning fires of my love,
I'd keep you,
Till you open your eyes,
and submit to my arrogance.

Mohammad Sammour

To My Own True Love

(For My Wife, Jan)

Will you let me be the one
That keeps you warm at night?
Will you let me be the love
To fill you with delight?
Will you let me be the love
That never gets in your hair?
Will you let me be the one
That goes with you everywhere?

Will you let me be the one
Full of tenderness and care?
Will you let me be the love
Who thinks you are beyond compare?
Will you let me be your love
Year after year after year?
Will you let me be the love
That goes with you everywhere?

Will you let me be the one
Who makes your favourite sarnie?
Will you let me be the love
That never acts crass or barmy?
Will you let me be the love
That's an everlasting passion prayer?
Will you let me be the one
That goes with you everywhere?

Will you let me be the one
That outshines every rampant Romeo?
Will you let me be the love
That never becomes a mindless moaneo?
Will you let me be the love
That knows you're kind and fair?
Will you let me be the one
That goes with you everywhere?

Will you let me be the one
That brings your morning cup of tea?
Will you let me be the one
That lets your mind roam wild and free?
Will you let me be a love
Like a bottle of wine so rare?
Will you let me be the one

That goes with you everywhere?

Will you let me be the one
That never ever snores?
Will you let me be the love
That never over bores?
Will you let me be the love
Who's just part of a marvellous pair?
Will you let me be the one
That goes with you everywhere?

Will you let me be the one
That rocks your favourite songs?
Will you let me be the love
Who will always right your wrongs?
Will you let me be the love
Your guard from verbal warfare?
Will you let me be the one
That goes with you everywhere?

Will you let me be the one
That lights you up like an old funfair?
Will you let me be the love
Who writes you lyrics like a French trouvere?
Will you let me be the love
To make your heart tap like Fred Astaire?
Will you let me be the one
That goes with you everywhere?

Will you let me be the one
That thinks of you as gentle and profound?
Will you let me be the love
To whom my heart is ever bound?
Will you let me be the love
Who can't stop shouting, 'Yeah! Yeah! Yeah!'
I know I will always be the one
To go with you everywhere.

DESMOND BOSTON

Today I Woke Up

Today I woke up, I looked at the world
All the colours and pictures were suddenly so vivid
I looked at my past when I was so alone
I was so caged in, there wasn't much fun
Then finally one day I met you.
My life started all over fresh and anew
You taught me to laugh again
Showed me how again, I could smile
You showed me that I could, take that extra mile
No matter how near, or how far, you made a difference
From that day forward, I woke up, I embraced the anew that day
You lead me down a new path, you took me a new way
Where I could see the world, how, things could really be
You showed me, that this is a happy place to stay
Where we could be content, so all I need to say
Whether it be short term or whether it be forever
It doesn't matter as long as I met you
If it may be short or long
Thank you for the moments we shared
It meant so much, knowing someone
Like you cared.

Karl Holloway

SAINT

She was nice and sweet too
She had the patience of a saint
Meals were always on time
She would always slip us a few bob when we were skint
When we got hungry sandwiches were always on hand
When we all drifted away as time went by
She would always call to see if everything was alright
When we came to visit she was so pleased to see us
But our blissful life came to an end when Alzheimers took her from us
We will always remember her as she was

A lovely wife and mother.

FRANK TONNER

Trying Times

2012, that one single year
has gone by since I met you.
I was alone in a hospital waiting room.
A small, very quiet, still place.
I was in the world of thought.

You came in, briefly, a middle-aged woman
wearing slippers and a dressing gown.
You quickly looked around, then left.
A patient, that's all, I thought -
My mind was on someone else.

Minutes later you came back
accompanied by a church minister.
Together you sat down on my right.
You began to speak to him -
Extremely personal.

'I was told I have terminal cancer
and there is no cure'
Your voice was calm.
'I am worried about my son,' you said,
'I think of my son . . .

He cannot cope with it
he has just changed job
he has a very busy, high-power job
I am worried about him,' you said.
Trapped in your own world.

Sadness within you, sadness.
I felt uneasy.
I felt a sense of wrong.
I was about
to stand up and leave

when the church minister suggested
with kindness and gentleness
'Shall we go out in the garden?'
You both stood up and left.
You shut the door behind you.

CLAIRE-LYSE SYLVESTER

I Gave Love A Chance

I gave love a chance
I gave it a try
Our love was strong
Then things started to go wrong
I knew that she didn't love me
She would cheat and lie

I gave love a chance
I gave it a try
We shared the laughter and the tears
We had a few great years
When I found out what she had done
All I could do was cry

I gave love a chance
I gave it a try
Believe me
It wasn't so bad
There were many great times we had
I just wasn't her guy

I gave love a chance
I gave it a try
Together we became one
But now that she has gone
I have so many memories
Of a lifetime that passed me by

I gave love a chance
I gave it a try
We were happy together
But nothing lasts forever
Everything must come to an end
It was so painful to say goodbye.

Michael McNulty

THE RETURN

He returned home after those rough war years
The way his father had returned home
After the stones of that other great conflict
The familiar things were still there
White cups
A brown teapot
Warm friendly chairs
And a floor scented with that same old polish
He remained silent though
As is the way
About the things he had seen
Silent as the soft slippers his mother still wore
But there is the occasional night
Day
When they rise up
To trouble him with faces
Long gone faces
And
Other
Things
He remembers then how he left home for foreign places
Leaving his mother standing at the door
Waving
Waving to her boy
A boy who slipped quickly into manhood
A boy who saw things his father had seen before
In another war
Another awful
Awful
War.

JOHN JONES

The Silence

The silence,
the calm, tranquillity and peace,
with the soul, the spirit and the mind.
Are part of the human and common sense,
which each person man or woman aspire.
That signific, each human being, are
able to live the life without anxiety.
And others type of fear and worry, that
obviously make the most independence
of so many people personal aspiration.
In this fast life, dynamic and actual of
the modern world of twentieth century.
Full of religious dispute, not human love.

The silence,
gave to all the way to live good life,
and to develop constructive programme.
It's extremely important, the human contact,
with several and various type of person.
Even, some time the human contact, it's
not genuine, real and natural at all.
In sense, to poison, the ambiance, the atmosphere,
which surround the area we operated.
Obviously, the air we normally breathe come
to us, polluted, numb and contaminated.
Unfortunately, we always receive surprise,
aggression and punishment in this today world.

The silence,
represent for us the real medication, the
drug which care the modern day of sickness.
The trench, who repair us and made shield,
at any moment to many infinity of dangers.
Although, for us very goodwill it's to
live in peace and harmony with the human being.
Included, all common people who live and
work in all the nations of the planet heart.

Which belong, at any ace, language, culture,
religion. And to people, with divers attitude.
In respect, we are not entitled to make any
judgement or to understand the silence of others.

ANTONIO SIGNORELLI

A Tiny Little Photograph

Today I saw a photograph
Just a snapshot of you and I.
A tiny little photograph
Though goodness me, it made me cry.
Just to see you as I loved you
And me here with my life complete
But how I loved you, did you know?
In fact it shook me to my feet.
It brought back the pain and anguish
From when I had to let you go.
Now you know I don't still love you
But how I loved you, did you know?
I haven't for such a long time
(And you have long forgotten me)
That tiny little photograph,
It simply jogged my memory.
And to see you as I loved you
It just had no reason or rhyme.
We have both changed and long moved on
And it's been such a long, long time.
I'd watch you whilst you were sleeping
And I could not have loved you more,
If your hair had hung down in gold
And it had reached down to the floor.
How I traced around your features
Whilst you were sleeping close to me.
I was completely mesmerised
Yes, caught up in your majesty.
Completely, I had forgotten
Yes, it was you that I adored,
Back then you were the world to me,
How I held you in high regard.
I thought I would always love you
Yes, from then to eternity.
Though sadly things did not work out
Do memories have perpetuity?
We now move different circles
On different merry-go-rounds
Forgotten about each other
And yes, new loves we have both found.
Just a black and white photograph
From before I became your wife

So strange to get a reminder
A freeze frame from part of my life.
Almost completely forgotten
How I could not have loved you more.
But to see you, as I loved you
I am so glad, once more I saw.
I would have walked through fire for you
To the end of the Earth and back
So sad that I had forgotten
Now I'll always remember that.
Just to see you as I loved you
Yes, I really, really loved you
And nothing can ever change that
No nothing we could ever do.

JANET EMERY

The Rough Ride

The wide open sea
Ocean waves so lovely
Bashing against the rocks
So pure and hard
Struggling on my yacht

I look to the sky
And pray
The Lord says to me
Be your best self
I try my cord every day

God answers
The waves go calm
No more danger for me

The path to my destiny
Starts right here
My struggle is over
I've won my life back
In society and community
Yes!
For the world
Is here just for me
To give and grow strong
With my own positivity.

Deborah Storey

THE LOTUS POND, BALI

The Bali garden is still and heavy with rain,
And moisture rises in gold-flecked columns
From the drenched earth as it breathes out
A deep rich fragrance on the air.
Jewelled frogs blink and woo amphibiously
In Karma Sutra poses round the pond,
And a watched snail on a varnished leaf
Can take a shining hour if done well.
Small doves croon from frangipani tops,
And the steam answers on the rocks below.
The lotus pond shines tourmaline clear,
And prisms flash on angled leaves.
Ancient stone animals crouch, pockmarked,
In shadows, scarlet hibiscus at their ears,
And above all this great showy flowers
Float and sway on sinuous stems,
The supermodels of the floral world.
In luminous Buddha pink they glow;
First the weighty buds, rich with promise,
Wrapped in pale green silk, and then
The strong veined petals slowly swell, break free
And open to the monsoon sun. Morning dew
Catches in the cup like quicksilver, slides about,
Until the flower bends, bows, tips liquid out
With a silent splash, swings up again,
Blushing at the sun. Call it an Ubud,
A liquid measure for the exact amount of rain
A lotus flower can hold, until it tips.

LIZ DAVIES

Story Of A Hometown

Once upon a life,
In a small, suburban town,
Where street lamps
Cried for light
When night crawled around.
In the dark
There began
A small hope,
The start of a new beginning,
In the falling cosmos,
Of beauty and dust.
Only there
Could hold the rebirth
Could turn the shadow,
Into the star of the night,
That would help others
Find their way home
Because they never could.

Chloe Harvey

WHY POETRY?

With linguistic gymnastics,
Communication's rations of passion
Leap, curl and unfurl onto pages,
Where joy, sentiment and rages
Can go on and on (sometimes wrong) for ages!
This is the poet's lot, his or her plot,
To change, arrange and rearrange life's pot
Of meandering circumstantial shots
At the human condition's clotted lot;
Nuances of difference compete in the heat to be hot.

I write to right things, to hinge the unhinged,
To question the essence of essence in binges
Of drills with skill into life's ills and fringes;
To bring potency to the impotence of language's words,
The absurd, the sublime in colourful whinges!

OSMIN M TURK

Berg

Thro' the spyglass I saw them
Twenty miles off the coast;
Each gliding o'er the ocean
With the grace of a shimmering ghost.
Snapped from their moorings with a single twist
Of nature's raw-boned hand and wrist:
With a roar they departed from their sanctuary shore.
Bergs like gigantic ice-sculptured swans
Silently swimming an eternal pond;
Pierced by a million arrows of light
Exploding in diamante frost drenched white.
Cracked meringues with their peaks and troughs
Created before man first made his clocks;
Prismatic statues refract Marian blue
As pure as an angel's soul thro' and thro'.
Behemoths, mammoths, bellicose masters
Tear open the throats of any tin canisters
Sailing into the throne room of kings.
Where the screams of hacked metal are heard on the strings
Of a siren's wind plucked harp;
Every shriek a clear note gutting blade sharp.
Yet, I know as they know, they drift to their end
Drawn on foam horses, by temperate forces
Thawing the bellies of leviathan prowlers;
Spewing over the water castanet growlers.
Echoes of clinking, clacking and chinking
The death throes of a berg with the bell buoy ringing.

Philip J Mee

MOONLIGHT UNLOCK

A rock pool meets the river again
Pours its soul back out to sea
Dust of Earth heads heavenwards
In stars that shine for thee
All is meant for someone
Whether in space or Earth
As your spirit pulls me in
With you I feel some worth

Celestial rays light a dungeon
A prisoner feels human
No tide would be at home
If it never returned to shore
Moonlight unlock the heart
Return her to this land
What purpose will I have in life
If she won't take my hand?

RODGER MOIR

The Moments Of Waiting

The song that I have sung in the past
remains unsung to this day.
I have spent my days in stringing
and in unstringing my instrument.

The time has not come true,
the words have not been rightly set;
only there is the agony
of wishing in my heart.

I have not seen thy face,
nor have I listened to thy voice;
only I have heard his gentle footsteps
from the road before my house.

But the lamp has not been lit
and I cannot ask him into my house;
I live in the hope of meeting with him;
but this meeting is not yet.

The time increases
its distance between itself and me,
I have only hopes in my heart
begging me to shorten the distance.

I shall be left all alone in the world
with the song being sung in my heart,
and loneliness to accommodate me
till the end of my breath.

Shabed Ali

TALKING TO THE DEAD

Wishing to reside here;
cooking with a covered clay pot,
spices used, as he had;
ginger, five spice, coriander,
Szechuan pepper imported from home.

I remember repeated instructions;
fry, toss, pour, toss and lid on,
never stirring, not knowing the consequences.
We waited with cigarette -
I would watch smoke leave his tar-stained teeth,
as he fiddled the loose one with his tongue.
We could talk here. Undisturbed,
no prying eyes on our secret debates.
Our hunger pangs disappeared with each simmering bubble -
sneaking bites out of the not-yet-ready meal.
Those minutes were quieter, just Frank Sinatra and him.

As I forgot not to stir, wooden spoon in hand
in a kitchen he's never been to,
this unfamiliarity returns -
dinner congealed, spoiled.

CHARMAIN LEUNG

Sins Of Our Behaviour

The effects of sin, those who have lied,
Have become deceitful,
Those who have stolen have become wanted,
Those who have fornicated, live in peril,
The Devil knows your game,
To live by the sword, is to die by the sword,
To live by the gun, is to die by the gun,
To live by ill-gotten gains,
Eventually brings torment,
A sinner never rests,
For the universe knows your mind,
If you carry on regardless,
Then happiness will be destroyed,
For a cheating heart will die,
So live a life of joy instead,
By being honest, benevolent
And respectful.

James S Cameron

GLUTTONY

The population of people today are greedy
They don't care about the needy
They always seem to want money
And want it in a hurry
I don't feel we need every penny that's in our pockets
People are stealing and killing for the love of it
Gluttony is up by the excess
Tell that to the rich
To the money-grabbing bastards out there
I say forget the materialistic things
And all the luxuries
I'd rather use my salary to see the Aborigines.

NATALIE PETERSON

Mum I Love You

Mum, I love you, I really do
Everything I am, I am because of you.

You taught me compassion at an early age
And been there for me through every stage.

School was a nightmare, I didn't fit in
I was so tall and they were all thin.

I wanted to be special, Daddy's little girl
I hated my straight hair, really wanted it to curl.

I loved you Mum while I was growing up
And really meant the word written on your special cup.

You were always there to listen, you never say I told you so
When there's something I don't understand, you say, 'Ask and I will show.'

We always laugh and giggle, I hate to see you cry
And Mum, I'm really dreading the day we have to say goodbye.

Oh Mum . . . how will I go on without my best friend?
All your hugs and kisses up to Heaven I will send.

I'll talk to you every day, I know you'll be close by
I'll miss you so much Mum, this is the reason why.

Mum, you've always loved me, you've held me as I've cried
Every time I've failed, you've smiled and said, 'At least you've tried.'

We walked along the path of life, you've always held my hand
You've told me no matter what, by my side you'd always stand.

You've never let me down, go hungry or feel the cold
And I truly hope God lets you stay till you're very old.

I'll become the one that will never let you down
I'll make sure you always smile, couldn't bear to see a frown

The years of love you've given me, the hours that you spent
The arms to always hold me, the shoulder you always lent.

All the love invested, the hours, minutes too
Now it's time, dear Mum, that I gave it back to you.

I hope you know how much I love you, I'm grateful for all you've done
The best day of my life was the day I got you as my mum.

ANGELA HENSLEY

Furrows And Poppies

In an English field beyond a five bar gate
Stands with the boughs outstretched
The iconic view of an English oak tree
Mighty and strong, straight and true
From these fields and estates many men and lads
Heard the tune of the piper and followed
Enlisted and marched off to foreign fields
The piper stood his ground from whence
He came, played the pipes – calling all to take
Arms and where he went they followed
For every ring of that standing oak stands
For two hundred lives – multiply it by
Age and growth a total sum of lives lost
In a country home beyond a lychgate stands
A churchyard and where the yew trees grow
Those who returned – were battleworn and lame
But this was war and no one was to blame
Beside the churchyard stands a vicarage
And on a late summer afternoon – air -
Refreshed after a thunderstorm -
One question lies unanswered – that of
War poet Rupert Brook (1887-1915)
Will there still be honey for tea?

David Charles

A Hard Road

Here they come, up
from depths of memory:
Tired sad teachers, who came
from war to command kids
they'd never understand.
The bullied and the meek
of school, irrelevant to
a bigger world they later joined.
That band, too weak
to know their minds,
as thousands of drones
to work their lives
in ordinariness.
Another generation failed
by their 'betters'.
As my poor mother.
Who couldn't like children
and didn't know love . . .

JOHN JUDD

Testing Time

I was learning to drive
And proceeded to strive
For success and I gave it my best.
But it soon became clear
That irrational fear
May prevent me from passing the test.

As the weeks rolled along,
All my efforts went wrong
And I feared what the test may entail,
As I couldn't recall
Any road rules at all;
I was scared that I'd possibly fail.

Then I broke down and cried
For, despite how I'd tried,
My manoeuvres were always a mess.
When he saw me, my dad
Said, 'What's wrong with you lad?'
Being challenged, I had to confess.

'Just be positive, son,
That's how battles are won!
If you're positive you can sail through it!'
Now today's the big day
And I'm able to say
That I'm ***positive*** that I can't do it!

Dennis W Turner

Thanks

Do you ever stop to think
About the food that is upon your plate?
As you sit down at the table,
To enjoy a meal,
Or the peaceful night's sleep,
That was full of only happy dreams
For the laughter of small children,
As they go about their play
To the fact that you woke up,
And get to live another day?
For all your friends and family,
Who remain faithfully by your side?
In spite of your flaws and faults,
Which they all abide?
So give thanks to those people,
And to everything you have,
For you are richer than you realise,
For as long as you shall live.

PAULINE UPRICHARD

From My Boy's Birthday

Long ago, on Roman Census night
With cold homes held in a cloak of white,
A babe was born in Bethlehem Town
As angels sang and a star shone down
Showing shepherds to a stable bare
To adore Christ in His parents' care.
Later with great gifts came wise kings three
To worship Jesus on bended knee.

Like God's creations beholding there
May we this Christmas praise Jesus, fair,
Who still brings love for the world to see
In each repeated Nativity.
Sadly, many years have since begun
And folks have turned from God and Son
Who could repent sin to hear Him say,
'You were forgiven from my Boy's Birthday!'

Ronald Rodger Caseby

COMMUTER MADNESS

I ran from the taxi, clumsy, rushed,
Far too many things that I need to beat
The fatigue, the dust, the curfew,
The din, the rush and the heat

I sit back in the train carriage
I leave the city hell at the ticket gate
I look at my watch. Pause for breath
And despair that things are running late.
I look back onto the platform

From the window it is all moving far away
Outside night closes in on a demanding city
Yet the city lights keep the sleep and dark at bay
A small jerk and we're moving

At last I reach my destination
At a quiet, deserted suburban station.
I see spots of light from windowpanes
Through dark and lonely country lanes

I see the light of a tavern, I think
Shall I pop in for one small well-earned drink
I become aware of my footstep being the only sound
Apart from a single dog walker I am the only one around

A few more streets left
A walk even blindfolded I know
Only one last effort for a tired heart, body and soul to go

STEVE PROUT

Fire Flowers

And only where the forest fires have sped,
Scorching relentlessly the colder northern land
A sweeter elderflower lifts its purpled head,
and like some gentle spirit sorrow-fed
It hides the scars with this heaving helpless hand.

And only to the heart that knows of grief,
of desolating fire, of human pain,
there comes some purifying sweet belief,
some fellow-feeling, beautiful, if brief
And life revives and blossoms once again.

And only when summer's breath has burnt itself out
will this fragile frame feel free in life's big file
A bittersweet birth will fill my mind once more
Like fire and ice which when this spirit stirs
But only where the forest fires have sped . . .

Judy Studd

Do The Maths

Some have the ability to see dead people.
Me . . . I see numbers . . .
Digits to be precise.
Last week whilst along Tatterman St . . . I saw a 5.
Later that day, I saw a 3 brazenly sitting at the bus stop.
A fortnight elapsed when I brushed past
An 8 at the local supermarket.
In the evening after leaving the snooker hall . . .
I encountered 3 sixes in the kebab house . . .
Curiosity finally got the better of me.
'Who are you?' I enquired.
In unison they turned as one.
Gazes fixed firmly upon me and replied . . .
'We Are The Sum Of All Fears.'

JOHN MCAULIFFE

Just A Boy

Fresh freckled face, tousled hair
Facing life without a care
Smartly suited, latest style
In the mirror glance a while
Rather liked what he could see
Innocent, footloose and fancy free
Just a boy

Is this the same young fresh-faced lad
Parading now in khaki clad
Striding with steccato tread
Proudly marching straight ahead
Tearful mothers view the scene
'My son is barely seventeen'
Just a boy

Laid low in trenches 'neath the ground
Death and squalor all around
Hungry, tired, no relief
Boyish face now etched with grief
Will this nightmare ever end
Why can't my foe become my friend
Just a boy

Forgotten now those days of youth
Those pretty girls, the odd half truth
A mother's love, a father's praise
And sometimes his reproving gaze
Memories buried in the fray
Now seem a million miles away
Just a boy

Cold the night, black the sky
Friends lie motionless nearby
Another hero for the cause
No trumpet sound, no wild applause
No cross to mark a young lad's grave
No epitaph to say how brave
Just a boy

Not for a him a second chance
Not for him a sweet romance
No wedding bells or Christmas tree
His children paddling in the sea
No future, nothing meant to last

Just a brief and transient past
Just a boy

On this sad day reflect with pride
Remember those who sadly died
And pray that peace some day will reign
Their sacrifice be not in vain
Just a boy
Just a boy
Just a boy.

GORDON WEST

No More Room (It Can't Just Be Me)

How I wish I had room in my cupboards,
For all the things I have got,
I'm scared to move some of the dishes,
Because I do have rather a lot.

How I wish I had room in my wardrobes,
Many clothes all squashed on a rail,
But to sort them out and throw some away,
Makes me quiver and go rather pale.

How I wish I had room on my shoe rack,
There are really too many pairs,
Some old for the garden, some new for days out,
And some . . . well they are just spares.

How I wish I had room on my coat rack,
There are eight double hooks on the wall,
Summer jackets, winter coats, various colours to choose,
But they've now taken over the hall.

One day I will have a clear out,
When I have some time to spare,
I just seem so busy with other things,
So spare time is really quite rare.

But which day will I choose for that clear out,
It will now have to be very soon,
I'll just fill some bags for a charity shop,
As I really have . . . no more room.

Elsie Kemp

In Memorandum

There is a karma,
Memory,
is its name.
It lives in that shadowland,
of restless sleep,
and fractured dreams.
In some dark cavern,
seeking pirate gold,
but finding not
Flint's treasure,
but a box, of Pandora's craft.
My name written,
in bold gilt.
Within, an infestation,
of mythical curse.
A lifetime's work,
of sin, disinterest,
neglect and cruel words,
angrily spat out,
never revoked.
All charged to my
personal account.
And memory,
has another name.
Title it: Hell.

STUART WRIGHT

Landscapes

The journey propels our traveller
towards a destination
across a landscape of people
and streets and fields and skies.
The mortal perceives the end
where all human journeys lead,
but fear obscures the awareness:

Not yet, not now, not here! . . .
I must abstain from exertion.
I must resist fatigue.
It's best to rest my eye
on the compass, and follow the map
that lists the famous sites,
that names the prime locations.

The landscape the traveller sees
becomes a tourist's passive
annotated map
for a recreational, footsore
adventure . . . yielding memories
too few, too faint to fill
a rainy afternoon.

Our journey propels a traveller
towards a certain end
across a landscape of people
and streets and fields and skies.
The grieving traveller perceives
too well the destination
awaiting every mortal:

I greet for the first and the last time
every creature I meet,
embracing with elation
even the lightest encounters.
I give myself to the joy
of this fleeting, graceful, one-way,
once-in-a-lifetime passage.

The passive landscape thus
leaps into life with passion,
and every greeting blooms
in the moment's eternity.
Notwithstanding the journey,
both the travellers must
meet their destination.

THOMAS LAND

The Sea

My grandson had never seen the sea before. I chose
This perfect heat-stained August day. He revelled in the

Treasures of the shore. He delighted in everything he saw.
And paddled in the ripples of the bay. My grandson

Had never seen the sea before. He heard a seashell echo.
Waters rear. And sifted sand from space to bucket. Play.

He revelled in the treasures of the shore. I hoard for
Home. I told him not to stray. My grandson had never seen

The sea before. I should have watched him more.
Carefully. Made sure I should have known that he would creep

Away. He revelled in the treasures of the shore. I knew
Before they gave up looking for him. My grandson had
Never seen the sea before. He revelled in the treasures
of the shore.

Imogene Lindo

My Fantasy World

Here inside my new home, falling into a dream.
Like Cinderella and Snow White.
As a child I would think about amazing stories
to tell my mum and dad every evening.
I would get so excited with the joy that follows
when my tales are read, they cry or laugh their feelings out.
In adulthood I really haven't changed much, holding onto my music
and poetry singing songs on holiday.
I can't leave my world of fantasy.
I feel no pain and feel no rain.
I feel the joy of life grow and fall deep in love with my surroundings too.
I feel so happy and resent the thought of never pulling away.
It is only when I close the door and lock the locks.
Do I leave my castle behind in snow and rain?
I have to make do to the unexplained truth.
Facing the cold reality; breaking away from my fantasy
from the outside world that engulfs me.
It's no Disney World
filled with difficult tests, challenges and harsh climate.
Until the day is over I return to my castle, this is the time I have.
The chance to be myself
comfortable and happy once again.
Sometimes writing my feelings down
writing poetry and song
capturing the day as it is
I guess I grew to believe in myself and see through the pain
of life and with my beautiful imagination I still continue to believe in happy endings.

NASSIRA OUADI

Sunflower

Morning sunshine, sparkles at the given hour,
All eyes travel to the awe-inspiring sunflower,
Dazzling and alluring, with a splash of brilliant yellow,
A flower with heart, which will continue to grow.

The sunflower will continue to smile and shine
Radiating love and strength, definitely one of a kind,
You are the centre, the glue and the heart,
My dear Alice, we advance with the love and wisdom you impart.

Kimberly Davidson

A Letter Of Proposal From A Secret Admirer

My dearest dear,
What you read, I am.
For I am no wealthy man.
I possess no diamonds, or rubies, or pearls,
But I am the self proclaimed lord of my own little manor (a bungalow)
My only other estate is a 'F' registration Hillman, 1968.
Jewels? Emeralds? Gold? Sapphire rings?
I have no wish of treasured things.
You see, I am no one grand,
But if you would kindly take my hand
I would be king of a vast empire
Of a land eternally green.
And you my dear,
My dearest dear,
You,
You then would be my queen.

PETER TERENCE RIDGWAY

Sinner, Or Saint?

As I wake, I think of you.
Only and constantly, you.
I long to be with you and stay in your loving presence.
My love. I must come to you today.
As I rise, I think of nothing but you.
You cover my every sense.
I will live my life just to be with you.
To love you. To know you.
To serve you.
I come to your home for I know you are there.
Always there.
And I feel your comfort.
I see your graceful form beckoning me.
I light a votive candle.
'Hail Mary, full of grace . . .'

Marco

MAIDEN OF VIRTUE

Virtuous is my name; virtuous is my nature!
Clothed in silk resistance
Bathed in pure blood,
None of thy stained soul.

Scorned and kicked
Whispered words
Left and dumped by men all alike

All alone remembering
When virtue was true
And heart was pure
Virtue was once more
Than virtue is now.

CHARLOTTE GERALDSON

Sinner Or Saint?

An Earthly island . . . ?
'Lost on my island?'
'Or is it a dream?'

I am lost on this beautiful island,
Oh what a sight, I am having the time of my life.
As the days go by, the sea waves show
And the winds from the breeze blows.
I can see the birds flying
And the weather is hot, so hot.
The palm trees are towering around the sea shores.
The fishermen are fishing,
And my love grows, all the more.
There are lots of exotic food to my heart's delight.
Do I want to be found?
I can see the beauty more,
When the day turns into night.

Yvette Avonda Layne

My Perfect Wife

My troubled life was torn apart on a very bright March day
I knew that something wasn't right and couldn't find the way
My marriage was in trouble but I struggled on in spite
When suddenly I realised, I no longer had a wife
She left me with two children, but didn't tell me so
I was left a shattered future without a word to show
My life with her was over, no word from her at all
But determination kept me going, I knew I could walk tall
And then my luck did change by chance, I met someone anew
Who took me with two children, and I took her two too
We met a lot of agro, they said we shouldn't wed
I didn't care, I loved her, since the two of us first met
After years and one more daughter, to make our lives so neat
Well now we've got to forty-one, the years that's passed complete
My wife is such a beauty, a blonde and blue-eyed mum
I'm proud to say she's all I want, forever and now on
We've had the lot thrown at us, but we managed to pull through
Two shattered lives that had no hope became a happy two
Mistakes are very often made, it really is just life
But after all is said and done, I've got the perfect wife.

Roy T Gough

Summer Holiday Thoughts

I spread my flowing gown across the blue sky
And in its folds toss my golden circlet.
My hair trails behind me, caressing flowers,
And enmeshes the raindrops in their fall,
As I dance, I sparkle in the depth of night
And sing lullabies to sleepy infants.
Suddenly the summer is here, but now,
My summertime celebration is complete.

Caroline Buddery

INTERVIEWS

I fail to see the bigger picture,
I lack enthusiasm and come across as cold,
My application forms are lacking with high powered examples,
Will I be promoted with one foot in the grave when I'm old?
I face stiff competition from much younger candidates,
The goalposts for the Executive Officer role I want have been raised,
Why didn't I apply for promotion in the past when things were easier?
With my failed interviews I am totally confused and dazed.
I was told that I would struggle if I applied for that Personal Assistant role,
An application form I sent has failed to pass the sift,
I'm trapped with no hope in my current role,
My self-esteem could do with a lift.
Maybe I'm only meant to be an Administrative Officer all my life,
With higher grade interviews I fail all the time,
I hope divine intervention will change my career for the better,
Then promotion one day will be mine.

FINE BULICIRI

Remember Me

Remember me as someone who
there in your life
was just passing through.
Remember me as someone who
always loved you along the way.

Remember me as someone who
loved every moment
shared with you
and if you asked me to
I would not a change a day.

Remember me as someone who
there in your life was
just passing through.
Remember us as someone who
always loved you along
the way.

K Lake

TRUE SPIRIT BUTTERFLY

True spirit butterfly of dusty blue,
Spring loves to open her door to you,
Nature loves you so very much
You love, the warm sun's kiss and gentle touch,
Your wings you open and close,
To keep you cool,
You love the light refreshing showers that fall,
The gentle breeze guides you along
Lifts you high and low
To the sweetest flowers that grow,
The gentle breeze blows kisses to you,
True spirit butterfly of dusty blue.

JOANNA MARIA JOHN

A Guiding Light

Remember the consultant,
Arrogance discarded?
Said his son liked the machines
Jostling his hospital bed.
'They sound like birds, Dad,' he'd said.

But perhaps I just dreamt it?
While floating in birdsong,
Passage light squaring room door.
I wish now I'd sung, not shouted,
'I'm really sick!' from my bed.

Dawn chorus falters, phoenix
Feathers flash! Gold ingot
Widens in the darkness.
Are angels in the doorway? No.
Said the doctor: 'You can go'.

Helen Poskitt

UNANSWERED

Why do I feel this way
I know she loves me
But why
I'm scared
I have changed
Why does she love me
Why does she love this monster
Can I promise her things will be different
Yes I can
Can I keep those promises
I do not know
I show love
Is it enough
Will she be there tomorrow
I can only hope
Seeing her smile makes me happy
I have seen this before
How long will it last
Moments
Will her love for me remain
Do I deserve her love
What have I done to deserve it
She has done nothing wrong
How is she still hanging on
Why do I feel she is going to leave
She is better off without me
After all I have put her through she is still here
Why can't I stop
Why am I this way
I hate it
I want to change for her
How can she love me
How can she love this monster
Hopefully there she will always be.

CHRIS TUCKER

Rocker Song

You are
a slice of spice, man,
but . . .
don't think
you can
soften me up
to break me down.

It ain't gonna happen

Don't think
you can
slap my wrist,
get my mind in a twist.

It ain't gonna happen

My sexual intrigue
is in a league
known only to me.

It ain't gonna happen.

You're listing my traits,
the gates of my mind
are open and free.
I'm not on the take.

You think I might break?

It ain't gonna happen.

Sally Plumb

HEATHER

A new day, a new dawn, a new sun in the sky
A new smile on your face for some lucky guy
As the world turns around we meet faces anew
Light shines in your eyes like the love you once knew
Come showers and raindrops like tears in your eyes
Sadness and sorrow, you had your goodbyes
So now a new day begins, keep that smile on your face
And make this old world a far happier place.

TREVOR A MERCER

Shadows

Shadows, in the still of night,
created by a clear moonlight,
silhouetted now the trees,
in the cool clear-nightly breeze,
shadows come and shadows go,
large distances some are thrown,
with light, reflecting behind them all,
whether they, be short or tall.

Some are round, while some are square,
look again, and they're not there,
see the shadows, changing shape,
as moonlight, now starts to escape.
Making way now, for the sun,
changing shapes, are now to come,
as morning arrives, a new form of light,
to cast its shadows, where it might.

Shadows moving, with changing light,
different shadows, than at night,
are seen once more, to reappear,
some hard to see, others very clear.
As night draws in, once again,
and with it comes the driving rain,
shadows fade, some right away,
until the break, of the bright new day.

When the sun, comes up once more,
after a good downpour, for sure,
shadows are forming, once again,
see the shadows, now of rain.
Rain on the leaves most every tree,
rain on most, to a degree,
then, as raindrops fall to Earth,
new shadows now, are given birth.

Stephen T Maslen

The Battlefield

A burst of machine gun fire ripped through the airless night,
The absence of wind caused every sound to magnify
And I crouched waiting,
Out there my enemy, whom I should be hating,
Grenades at hand, limbs tensed ready
The first line manoeuvres forward,
My brow is hot and my hand's unsteady,
The signal is given and a prayer is sighed,
Kill or be killed, yet I could have cried.
I ran like the wind in a hail of fire,
A comrade crumpled by my side.
I faltered to save him
In vain I tried;
A voice of command seared me through
Keep going I'm watching over you,
I saw a wounded face flash by,
There but for the grace of God go I,
A hand gripped my arm and dragged me on,
And at last the enemy were gone!

Beryl Skinner

True Life

My life began many years ago,
Where it would lead me really didn't know,
At school fourteen years old and never been kissed,
Until then I didn't know what I had missed,
Years went by, we were married with a family of three,
My school love was still faithful to me,
We worked hard through thick and thin,
I couldn't imagine my life without him,
But then sixty years on,
My true love now had gone,
He is still looking down from above,
I close my eyes and feel his love,
I never knew how much I would have missed,
If I hadn't surrendered and been kissed.

Diane Young

STAR GAZING

When we see the sun sinking in the western sky,
We know that the stars will come out very soon,
Glittering as they illuminate the heavens,
As we see them dancing with the moon.

In the darkness the majesty of the universe is displayed,
Stretching far beyond the limit of Man's imagination,
And knowing that space is constantly expanding,
The vastness of the heavens is beyond our comprehension.

Whilst there is so much we can do upon the Earth.
There is little we can do in outer space,
We may send rockets to the moon or other planets,
But this could be of little value to the human race.

Whilst we survey the night sky in all its majesty,
And recognise the other planets spinning many miles away,
We should remember that the Earth is our inheritance,
And it is this which requires our protection every day.

For we have been warned of the effects of global warming,
And that the environment is something we must protect,
That it is being destroyed by our present mode of life,
And that everything we do is having an affect.

Star gazing might be a very pleasant pastime,
But it is the life we live on which we must concentrate,
We must do all we can to protect the environment,
For it is this which will decide our descendants' fate.

RONALD MARTIN

Mam

Mam, you mean the world to me.
You were the head of our family.
We had our ups and downs.
We had laughter, tears and frowns.
You always told me I had to share.
I always knew you cared.
No matter how near or far
You will always be a shining star.

Elizabeth Riggott

My Life Is So Lonely

I feel so alone
The love that I had has forever gone
The one that I loved is with me no more.

How can this be?

I thought together forever
But that is no more
He will always be with me
But not as before
That life has gone forever.

So what do I do?

The man I once loved and knew is gone
This I can't accept
That together forever will be no more
My love, my life is over.

Where do I go from here?

All I know is I am lost, lonely and sad
Without me here who would cope?
I want to disappear, go away, forget
Maybe one day soon that will be
Right now I can't wait
To go and meet my date with fate
And really be no more
I've lost my love, my life
Maybe now's the time to close the door
And leave this life behind
My mind is a mess, this I must stress
So don't be sad, the time has come
For me and my lost love to be as one.

Goodbye, please don't cry.

I will be at peace with my one true love
Goodbye.

L Edwards

Guardians Of The Soul

There are strange beings, of the night
That we may not behold
Don't be afraid . . . they guard our dreams
If we dare to be bold.
These are creatures of darkness
And are there to console
Between those hours, of dusk and dawn
Guardians . . . of the soul.
They are there, to protect us
Hovering, beyond celestial spires
Driving away, soul collectors
Who feed on our desires.
And these sacred deities dwell
On a very much higher plane
They are the eyes, of our sleep nights
And when the moon, is on the wane . . .

These beings are our consciousness
Our heartbeat, our breath,
Because of them, our souls live on
Even after death.
Our guardians of the soul
With the demons eternally fight
Holy riders, of another realm
Holy riders, of the night.
As we sleep . . . in innocent slumber
Unaware, of the evil beyond
The evil waits to steal our souls
And into the night, abscond.
But our ever, unseen guardians
Are waiting, for the black entities to begin
And our souls are always saved
From the Devil within.

Dave Kwiatkowski

WRITING

Words come over me
Like the ocean crashes over the rocks
Like the spray
Throwing my emotions in the air
Falling like confetti
Landing wet upon the page.

I paint pictures with my pen
Colours bright
And shadows deep
Showing your reflections
In the mirror of the page.

Stacking up emotion on emotion
Reaching out and touching
That tender spot so guarded
With the feather of my quill.

KELVIN KRIESCHER

Animal Party

It was the night before Christmas,
The snow was gently falling down.
Everything was covered white
In the woods, it was decorated around.
All around, an oak tree, animals so small
Footprints of little rodents, rats and mice
Were sitting, waiting on the ice.
Rabbits arrived, hopping everywhere
Hedgehogs formed a prickly line
Toads sat on large toad stools too
Snakes wriggled along the ground
Birds perched on branches all around
Then came a very, very loud sound
Cymbals clanged, drums banged
Then deer, fawns, badgers and bears
They all danced together there
This was their Christmas party.
No humans allowed.
From the smallest ant to crawl
Dancing, prancing up the tall trees
Lizards, grasshoppers hopping around
To the big drums' sound.
The woods were alive that night
What a spectacular sight
A great Christmas do
It's such a shame
They didn't invite you.

Trudie Sullivan

GRANNY'S HOUSE

you told us not to play inside
but we still went a little wild
we broke lots of your things
your tights were ropes and
bannisters were swings
we broke your ornaments
I don't know if you knew
if you did you never shouted
left us to fix them up with glue
and when the glue ran out
we used chewing gum instead
it didn't really matter
you still kissed us before bed

and when our house of cards came down
we still had your home
my heart has always stayed there
I still miss the breakfast bowl
you set out before you slept.

KESHIA STARRETT

Married To A Ghost

I went to a funeral yesterday
It was my great aunt Kate's funeral
You know what funerals are like, you wear something black
You meet long-lost relatives, sing a few hymns,
Have a drink with them and say your goodbyes . . .
That's it really, the essence of a funeral . . . until the next one.
As a child my dad told me that she was married a long time ago
But her husband had died.
No, he didn't die, well technically he did,
He was ***killed*** fighting for king and country.
They had only been married a year.
She grieved, she wore widows weeds but she never re-married
In her eyes she was still married
She saw him everywhere, spoke to him when no one else could listen
As she grew older, he never did
No one had the heart to tell her that she was married to a ghost . . .

Ray Tough

HARPOONED

Moving moodily
Through the waters,
Dark with depth
Shiny as jet,
On the flap of flukes;
Breathing laboured
After an hour down;
Then luxuriating
In the Arctic air:
No premonition
Of the gun's crack,
The harpoon's smack
And the inconsolable pity
Of the death groan.

DAVID BURL

Historic Move

Making history, Scotland on the move,
May the discussion be for the best!
With different values and ideas,
On the outcome, stand together final Quest!

Nessy with bags packed ready to go,
As everyone had a right to their say.
Voted for freedom and the chance to share,
Is Nessy's journey and destiny your way?

But will the borders be closed?
And others queuing to escape?
With passports and visas at the ready,
Plus duty frees, as a visitor's bait?

Restrictions and new laws to learn,
Exports and imports with a different view.
The exchange rate, what's money worth?
Work permits, hurdles to achieve the new!

Or working together and sharing tasks,
Must be the foundations to success?
Supporting each other in government and sport,
So why should we all settle for less?

Saw Nessy on the move,
No passport or visa to the kingdom.
Something tells you the outcome,
Nessy, like others loves our freedom!

Ann Beard

Silken Lady

Burnished cannibal
sun touched
climbs down her ladder

exhausted builder
sleep wheeled
waits for a husband

hunched like fudge
weaves a coffin
opening this grave.

Medieval city glistens
angel at centre
paved steel lines – he treads

between bronze skeletons
dangling to surrender
upside-down waiting

silken legs moving
slowly, gift is offered
accepted, he climbs on board.

TETA

July 2014

Frying, baking, grilling, toasting -
All descriptive of days
When I feel as though I'm roasting -
Exposed to the sun's rays.
Near and far, objects are dazzling -
But I can feel my brains frazzling . . .

Though, feebly, managing to plead:
'Idiot! Find shelter!
Such urgent advice you ***must*** heed.
At midday, ***don't*** swelter.
Believe us, you'll find it no joke
If you are stricken with sunstroke!'

About white beaches and palm trees
From now on I'll not dream.
All I want is a cooling breeze,
Not a tan or suncream
NOT to become a grease spot here . . .

'I'm home! Please – a ***drink***, cold and clear.'

Christine Mary Creedon

21ST CENTURY GUISE

Religion no belief of mine
Lost in time
Fanatics with no human trait
Corroding the world with hate,
Disguising the power of life
Christianity in strife,
A million questions cloud my mind
No answers to truth can I find,
No words can define
The treatments of mankind
Over 2000 years of humanity
Life has turned to insanity,
Religion a cover-up
Within its fold
With no intent to clean souls.

BARBARA R LOCKWOOD

Dawlish Beach In August

I stroll down Dawlish beach in August
finding it hard to envisage the brutal winter storm
that severed the artery of the railway.
The tide is advancing: the moon
drags the sea's blanket back and forth,
foam as white as swans laps at my feet,
there are fishermen on the causeway now
as a gentle breeze caresses my brow

and Northern pensioners admire the view.
The sky is painted an Arabian azure
and stars seem to shine on the sea swell
in the serene somnolent ocean.
My glance holds Boat Cove and Coryton Cove,
on the other side Dawlish Warren and Exmouth
and I imagine I see a dinosaur's ghost
on this spectacular Jurassic coast.

A train thunders into the tunnel
on this wonderfully precarious line,
I admire the hole in the cliff
and the strange shapes of other ones:
one like a face, another an ant hill.
My troubles have ceased to haunt for a while
and there's a picture of awe on my face
as I marvel at this beautiful place.

Guy Fletcher

TIME

If you could picture time as a concept
To control our willing self
Would its beat change as our minds slept
Propaganda sold as health.

Time is an aid to healing
Advice for emotional pain
But how can it manage the feeling
To protect and keep us sane.

So how much time is for the living
An algorithm to measure breath
Age a counter for the reaper's ring
Taking us close to the time called death.

ALLEN SMITH

A Fairy Tale

Once upon a time, a newly married pair
Vowed they would be, forever happy and carefree
Through the years, they would drift, free from care
All problems they would solve so easily.

A very simple-minded couple were they
Yes, they were in cloud-cuckoo land
To think they could stay forever that way
And life would always be so grand . . .

They decided on two children, a boy and then a girl
But when a girl came first, they did not care
Their next was bound to be a boy, to set their hearts awhirl
Yes, they were all set for a pigeon pair.

They were vaguely disappointed when another girl arrived,
But still with spirits high, they both agreed
A third child, would not see them both deprived
So joyously awaited the next happy seed . . .

To be planted in their perfect and happy life.
Three children later, and all girls, left them slightly peeved,
True, there was no other trouble and strife
So they were certain one day, a boy would be achieved.

Their fourth embarkation, a girl yet again
Gave this slightly bewildered couple, food for thought
Would it be so very much a pain . . .
And would they be so very overwrought?

So, a fifth baby, they decided to conceive,
Yet another girl, left them reeling . . .
'For goodness sake,' said the wife, 'we'll have to leave
It at five' . . . though without much feeling.

So . . . determined still, an even number they chose;
'twoud be their lucky number six
But another girl was added to their woes
And it really got on their wicks.

Disheartened and angry, they decided to quit;
And then a nasty bombshell was disclosed.
For the wife nearly took a fit
When a letter came and exposed . . .

An affair her husband had, yielded a bonny baby boy
And this had left him shaking with laughter.
'Eureka!' he cried – she should call him Roy
And all concerned, lived happily never after.

DELPHINE

Off To War

A letter arrived for me today,
I've been conscripted to go to war they say,
To fight for King and this pleasant land
And to follow the regimental band,
Overseas in far off lands,
Killing with guns and with our bare hands,
Five long years we have fought in this war,
So now they have surrendered,
As scores of men have died so far,
So now on this Armistice Day,
We remember all the heroes we lost in the fray,
They were so brave and gave their whole,
For liberty of their country's soil,
We will always remember and will never forget,
All the brave men and women and those still fighting yet,
We humbly beseech you Lord God above,
Please send down your peace and everlasting love,
Grant us freedom from all conflict and war,
Let peace reign on this Earth for evermore.

Roy Muir

Baby Girl

Dry your tears baby girl,
There's no need to cry.
No matter what we haven't got, we still make it by.
Dry your tears baby girl,
For now we will pray,
And hope to God our luck will change,
We must just wait for the day,
Dry your tears baby girl,
And rest your weary head,
For now just use this stone cold pavement,
As we haven't got a bed.
Dry your tears baby girl,
I'm here by you,
In our final seconds we have together
I whisper 'I love you'.

JAY SHELLITO

The Road Reptile

Slowly it lumbered up the incline
rumbling into view,
angling steeply round the corner,
snoring as dragons do.

Its mouth on one side
now opened wide
sucked me into its belly,
where I joined the rest
making the best
of things, shaking like jelly.
The road-calming hump
made everyone jump.
It was noisy and smelly.

'Hello! How are you?' the usual greeting
got things under way.
Talking and smiling we journeyed onward
as we began to sway.

The beast began growling,
belching and howling,
clawing its way through the town.
There was no question -
it had indigestion!
All of us started to frown!
It coughed and it spluttered
and everyone muttered
'It's going to let us down!'

Somehow it reached the end of the journey
giving a mighty hiss!
We tumbled out giving our 'thank yous' -
blowing the driver a kiss.

I shot out like a weasel
into the diesel
and found a hanky to burrow

I must not make a fuss
about an old bus
But rather regard it with sorrow.
The hedgerow wrecker -
the double decker -
I'll need it again tomorrow!

DORIS R TOWNSEND

Delicate

Crushed into my palm
The rose, the thorn
You've forced the wound to bleed
To blister into my soul
When I begin to die
You peel the dead petals from my body
Watch me turn blue
As I shiver into the soil

You drink my tears
Catch my blood in a pipette
Boil my saliva on a silver spoon over burning charcoal
Then watch my shadow decorate into dirty ash
Lit a match, enlighten a candle
Your breath is so relaxed
Mixing my lust with melting wax

Vines twine inside my heart
I am suffocating
I am starving to hate you
But it's too late
You already own my love
Signed it with nectar dust
I tried to run
I tried to fight
But once you tattooed your name onto my tongue
I became transfixed with your taste
Wanting more and more of your sweet delicacy
But it was fake
Now I am to blame
I am too deep, tangled in your game

Onion skin
You pick at me to see what is inside
The acid stings your eyes
Trying to kill my spirit from being alive
Trespassing your lies
You want me
But confused
The fantasy is delirium
Guilty needle you inject your pain
Who is left to shame
Rusty nails grind into my bones
Your cold hands control

Digging my grave with sharp affection
I wait for my last gasp of air
While you seal my sight shut with glue
Closed my coffin
Goodnight.

EMILY RYDER

The Fens

Norfolk to Lincolnshire, that bitter North Sea.
The Wash of marsh and sickly salt air.
Bogged down with water, mud ploughed land.
Timid birds descend its plains.
Whistled wind passes the ice cold tip of noses.
Shelter from elements on this flat land.
For miles and miles, no spoilt view.
Ever changing from season to season,
Never stopping to pass a care.
The Fens' tempo remains relaxed and slow,
But mighty men had built this soil.
Like a yeasty spread, this shire can be loved or loathed.
Those born here cannot decide.
For country folk,
This is home.

Joseph Lowe

BOREDOM

Sometimes we'll let out a yawn
And there are many reasons why
We start to yawn from when we are born
And continue until the day we die

Though what is it that makes us stretch away
Is it due to lack of sleep?
We can yawn whether working or at play
Our eyes feeling very deep

And if we attend a seminar or speech
At times our boredom will show
No matter what they are trying to teach
Do we really want to know?

Boredom can set in at any time
It's so easy just to slip away
Life is precious until our very last chime
We should appreciate it night and day.

ANDREW EVZONA

The Rosary

The Catholic soldier on the Somme,
His rosary in his jacket pocket
To protect him from sudden death.
He and 60,000 others went over the top
On July 1st, 1916.
He had barely put his head
Above the parapet
When he was shot through the head,
And slumped back into the trench.
His rosary given him by Father Brian,
Back in Lancaster,
Lay scattered and broken in the mud.
It was one of the blackest days in the history
Of the British Army.

First of all,
There was the allied bombardment.
For seven days and nights they pounded
The German positions with heavy howitzers.
'Nothing can live under this bombardment,'
Their officers told them.
Unbeknown to the British,
The Germans had dug 70 foot deep shelters
In the chalk.
They put up banners saying: 'Come on!
We are ready for you!'
When the British infantry went in,
The Germans emerged and mowed them down
In their thousands, with machine gun fire.
40,000 lay dead and 20,000 wounded.

Liam had a girlfriend in Lancaster.
A car drew up with uniformed men in it.
She guessed what the news was.
'He died like a true soldier,'
They told her.
Beside herself with grief,
She went to Father Brian.
He gave her a rosary
To replace the one lost in the trenches.

The Royal Lancaster Regiment played the
Last Post at Liam's funeral.
Jennie never married again.

She witnessed Armistice Day,
November 11th, 1918
When Germany was finally defeated.

R O'SHAUGHNESSY

Purple Stars

For years she sat in the corner of time
like Master Horner of nursery rhyme.
Bearing neglect and solitude,
over attention with fortitude,
until that day the party started
and from her former life she parted.
Spiky purple stars came out
making all the people shout.
Wise men came with open books,
shaking their heads with knowing looks
as they marvelled at the sight,
trying to get their facts just right.
Millennium magic, we might have missed her,
Abracadabra pert Aspidistra.

Shirley Ann Johnson

MY WORLD

In my world there is you and me,
and everything is just fine,
with lush green fields,
where white cotton clouds just splash the blue sky.

In my world we can sing and dance,
and have fun all day long.
We walk together hand in hand,
until all the day is done.

In my world, when it gets dark,
I will walk you safely home,
and you definitely would love me
in the same way that I would love you.

So, in reality, it is cold and dark,
and the sky is grey and very dull,
but when our paths cross, you do not see me,
because you just see straight through me.

So, in truth, things do not work out,
as I am here on my own,
and there is no laughter in the world.
There is also no loving home.

So, now back to my world.
All I do is sleep and dream
of the day that I can make my world
be the same as your reality forever.

KEVIN GRIEVESON

The Horror Of War

A sea of red pains our eyes,
And the haunting chanters fill our ears,
But the passing of time,
Will not quell our tears,
A hundred years on,
And the wounds are still raw,
We cry for our dead,
That's the horror of war,
Oh when will it cease,
As we pray for peace,
Will it all end,
So we have no more graves to tend.

John Rookes

STARS ZODIAC

These are the twelve signs of the zodiac . . .
Look to your star, it just might tell you where you're at.
There is Capricorn as solid as a rock.
There is Aquarius, do not mock.
There is Pisces, oh so loving and giving.
There is Aries, full of war and so much more.
There is Taurus, what a bull at a gate
But not full of hate, like so many more.
There is Gemini, those who we do rely upon,
Sometimes it makes us one.
There is Cancer, homely and sound,
But sometimes cannot stand the crowd.
There is Leo, oh what a leader,
If you meet you will surely know.
There is Virgo, so kind, but nervous,
You will have to earn their trust.
There is Libra, oh so loud,
But beyond that facade they are so proud.
There is Scorpio, well hey ho, let's go.
They are so astute, with their world full of hope
But not least there is Sagittarius;
What a star they will go far do not mess, just caress.
These are my twelve signs of the zodiac,
If you disagree, please get back.
No one can ever be right, not all of the time.
So I say, as you may yourself,
Do not be left on that shelf . . .
Look to you and you will know what to do,
Put your (demons) to bed, enough said.

WENDY DEAVES

Me

Female being, sun and moon,
lonesome for Earth's song, her fuel.

Spirits of the universe are coming to me,
imagination, my cup of tea.

Feelings, intuition, sight and smell,
opens the flower, the tell.

Come ye children of system and rule,
follow the love inside your school.

Balance between the left and right will
cure the world of our civilisation's blight.

Each heart that soars into the light
creates the roars of happiness tonight.

My purpose to spread the feeling through
sound, sight and mind as tool.

I take this journey into my healing hands to replenish
the spirits, the life force, the lands.

Olwyn Morris

WHAT'S IN A FACE?

To glimpse a face, to glimpse a frown,
Sometimes up, sometimes down . . .

The smiling face hiding anger within.
The youthful expression of a phantom clown.
In shades of light a tear unfolds
Beckoning comfort the usurper looks down.

Eyes that laugh to a mouth that sees
The lips of youth shouting like tropical trees.
Facing the front the head of the class
Expressive by emission as nerves take their toll.
Reading Shakespeare by role; it was never this droll.
A goal has been scored on the pitch by the lake.
The keeper surrenders with a grimace to forsake.
Yes, in a face, in a frown, a face can behold
Knowledge of its keeper, if 'he be so bold'.

DAVID CHARLES

A Happy Poem

I need a little time -
let me be empty,
then float me back,

To beaches where Daddy, my daddy
builds sandcastles in the sky,
and high up my brothers play.

Mother watches us
we can run as far as she can see.

A thousand grains of sand
is the flavour of the beach,
the excitement fizzes over
into this life,

then I stick it down
in a book, pin it there.

Fíona Donaghey

Stepping On Your Words

Stepping on your words,
It's easy isn't it,
Stepping on your words.

All you need to do is step,
Step, step on the porcelain glass.
Smash, break, obliterate the fragile designs apart.
Pick, throw and kick the ceramic piece to destruction,
Because enough is never enough.
Enough is never enough.

Stepping on your words,
It's easy isn't it,
Stepping on your words.

All you need to do is step,
step, step into the blazing desert you create around us.
Lift, swipe and kill those you torment with the sword of your ice cold heart.

They ask why?
They ask why? They ask why?
None respond.
None respond. None respond.

Even in time, there's no resolution.
Even in time, there's no happy endings.
Even in time, the candles have blown.

In the dark, isolation has welcomed us in.
In the dark, we seal our secrets.
In the dark, fear gnaws into our living flesh.
Fear gnaws so heavily into us.
So heavily.
We are . . .

Consumed
Directionless.
Wounded.
Dead.

HAMDI SUFI

Winter Mountain

Cold, dark, silent and deep,
There she lies in wistful sleep.
Watched over by her guardians of light,
The heavenly stars and the moon now setting late at night.
Who with his parting yawn is gone,
Under the dark silhouette of the distant horizon.
His glow ebbing slow while the deep shadows shallow and shroud,
The vast empty spaces beneath their cloud.
Sun now rises to set his stage,
And calls for wind to send his message,
To all that now it is his day and all shall bow,
To every ray of his golden tide,
As it seeps into every cranny, nook and hide.
And so she wakes to brilliant clear blue sky, where,
First she takes her breath of crisp, fresh air.
Then stretching out her great strong arms,
She welcomes all to her modest charms.
The young and careless full of heart that knows no fear.
The old and wise with weakened eyes who hold their lives so dear.
They do not see beneath her veil of snow.
That look which hides her true character below.
But still they go in search of Heaven only to find,
They wind up in Hell as they fall for her gaping deeps.
Their echoes sounding out the bell of toll she keeps.
At eventide one can hear her cry,
For all those who now within her lie.
Deep, dark, silent and now cold,
Their souls imprisoned in her hold.
Till when she'll set them free,
On those long, dark, lonely winter nights to keep her company.

Donald C MacNab

A Fairytale Dream Delights

There it sits the dreamy moon,
A silver stream where little lovers swoon.
The depths of a sweet morello cherry sky,
Sailing midnight picnics aboard paddleboats as they up and fly.
A jolly jester at the helm,
A dotty dolly and a teddy toy.
With wishing rods cast out to fairy-realms.
Plotting joyful notes in the constellations high.
From ancient stars,
The carriage a fine ship soars.
Wild cinnamon horses and on they pull to far off shores.
Their coats as muscovado sugar,
Like angel hair their manes.
There it travels swift and light as feathers,
The vessel turned night-train.
Whilst magic elves spin the rigging,
Lift the sails across a star-filled night.
A beaming beauty helps turn the wheel to little lands far and wide.
Where small, quaint houses,
Abstract cottages and fairy castles up and rise.
A fairytale dream delights.
The magical wonder of the night.
Sweet dreams, goodnight.

Natasha Georgina Barrell

Love, Hope And Work

Love, we all think we need
by day and week
love of every type
without hype
many never achieve
not so easy to receive.

Turn to hope
hope for dope
hope for a load
hope for love
which will never come
Hope for other crops.

Hope dies
Love cries
Life suppressed
nothing left
feeling repressed
find work!

Mood depressed
well-dressed
well fed
well spoken
well-educated
Just work till you drop

Flight of thought
calmness bought
years gone by bring taut
dead heart without word
withered soul from work
is that it – all finished!

Renate Fekete

Grief

Swirling vortex of blackened anger
Rage burns and threatens eruption
Coiled springs awaiting release
Fingers clenched and ready to strike
But I hold back
Does anyone care about my pain?
Will I spend my days in gripping loneliness?
I do not know what I want to do
Who I want to talk to, where I want to go
I am losing my mind and the process is slow
I have no patience and if I get through today
What the hell do I do tomorrow?
Every day is different yet the same
Mundane chores and senseless TV
People see bereavement, they no longer see me
I am the person I have always been
But I am different, will I ever return?
Acceptance is something I have to re-learn
If not, my days will be dark and my nights forever long
A living country song
I smile, not with my eyes, I speak without a sigh
Sun will rise again tomorrow
I'll give life another try.

LYNN NOONE

Buoys

I want you to hear this later
Once I have opened my eyes
from beyond the buoys
where the big waves break
and their wet hands pull me
into a rolling swell
When I can be sure
you'll hear the telltale signs
of the water in my voice
before you call off the search
Knowing my boat is out there
and knowing that
I had not taken my best rope
I am not careful
I can only hope that in the wreckage
my little wooden apologies
will float long enough
For you to understand them.

Will Ritson

THE TRAIL

Despite the cursed winter chill,
As snow on snow dropped thick and fast
In haste decided, took the hill,
Then homeward as the twilight passed.

From ancient times the trail incised,
Had shortened out the journey quite,
But in this fall, was it so wise
To quietly go into the night.

On either side, the wooded slough,
Ice-capped pond and sluice gate wheel.
And cutting through beneath each bough
Moonlight caste . . . the trail surreal.

The wind took up in gusting squall,
Which hard did take my stride astray,
And snow with snow did drift and fall,
In vast enchanted roundelay.

Thicker now the flakes and cold,
My eyes asquint my chilling face,
Could Wenceslas have been so bold,
The trail grew dim and hard to trace.

I wandered lonely as a fox,
About the even crisping snow,
Until the navigation locks,
I caught askance and down below.

Against the frosted village light,
At once the trail came into view,
Trodden down and sparkling bright,
Nearer now, oh God bless you!

ROGER MOSEDALE

Thankful Thoughts 2013

I am so very grateful, that our family's fit and strong,
There's so much sickness in the world, which always seems so wrong.
I'm so impressed with people, whose lives are torn apart.
Their grit, and determination, truly touches your heart.

I've seen lots of broken families, through divorce and drugs and drink.
It makes some of us more careful, and really makes you think.
Illness creates harsh barriers, no work, no cash, no hope
Poor diets, or bad parenting, when it's very hard to cope.

Most of all, I am so thankful, that because we have our health
We can work, have hobbies, and a different sort of wealth.
My wife and I are happy, we have a wonderful group of friends.
We think the world of all of them, and hope it never ends.

Living in this country, with our changing seasons now,
Autumn colours and landscapes just make my heart go 'Wow'.
Misty mornings, golden sun, winds gusting through the trees.
Sights, almost religious, makes you fall down on your knees.

Music, and dancing is like manna to my soul.
Makes me smile, and happy, and fitter on the whole.
Our grandkids keep us moving, we love them all to death,
So that we can have these grateful thoughts, every time we take a breath.

Brian Hurll

HEALING

O' energy, of the universe,
healing me within.
The church is against it
but is Reiki actually a sin?

A healing miracle, a knee so cured,
all the pain gone, I endured,
Walking free
my wholesome healed knee.

I am actually healthy
Reiki waves are cleaning and healing
a miracle of positive energy
wellness and wholesomeness.

CHRISTOPHER GILLHAM

Dream Machine

Snow fell softly, easily, as I walked into the wild wood.
Flakes freckled my skin, like the gentlest touch of a swan's wing.
All about me carousel swirls of white speed through the silence of night like whirling dervishes.
A lonesome owl hoots from atop a black spindly pine,
Its branches drooping under a blanket of snow in the darkness surrounding me.
Afraid, I cling to the Sequoia's trunk like a white witch hugging a tree as shadows shift weirdly in the moon's silvery light.
Alone with my fear, a sudden sound of laughter caught my ear as the moon slipped behind a demon cloud.
I peered through the branches to see a circle of light form a ballroom of icy white, pristine, unseen by any other being.
There a young girl danced in circles, toes tiptoeing in the air.
As snowfall enveloped her head I noted her frosty lashes, her cool blue eyes, was she real, was she alive or dead
In the eeriness of winter I watched enchanted as snowflakes tickled her nose,
Then she rose into the rimey air as if by magic.
Her laughter echoed through the wild wood as she held her arms up to the starry sky;
The moon slipped behind a wispy white diaphanous cloud, and for a moment silence reigned.
As the moon loomed forth, the girl with the golden hair floated back down into the space, a bewitching smile on her luminous face.
Ghostly apparitions of wolves appeared at her side, as they howled their haunting song to the moon it echoed through the pines burdened with snow, and I was lost in a dream with nowhere to go.
The wolves' misty muzzles danced at her side, their amber eyes afire,
She turned in a circle as they pranced all around, and the bony handed skeleton made not a sound.
I peered around me as ghoulish arms encircled her hair, and light as dandelion down she was lifted into the air.
Headless now she danced to their tune, drifting like a puff of smoke as she rose with them into the depths of velvet blue, the sunken eyes staring as she flew.
A chill penetrated the night, and her head spoke spookily as if she knew I was there.

I heard, fly with me, fly with me, as a ghostly hand reached out, and like a view into another world, the frost unfurled.
Would I to be lifted above the cold cold earth, to somewhere or nowhere, another birth.
Was I, I wondered where I had not yet been, or tell me was I a dream-machine?

JENNIFER H FOX

The Autumn Chill

There's a chill in the air
autumn has arrived.
The leaves are changing to
red, orange, yellow and brown.
Berries too as red as can be,
to feed the birds as the frost comes down.
They will be happy as can be that we may feed them,
to keep them fed, and help them keep warm
in this autumn chill . . .
They give us pleasure in so many ways.

Anita C Walker

WRAITHS

We tread this way but once, I'm told,
Who said it, I'm not sure.
But some return – that I do know,
I've seen them cross the floor.

Heard them in the woodwork -
Beneath the boarded ground,
Smelled the wraiths within my house,
That unearthly,eerie sound!

Sat up and felt them in the room,
That shiver down the spine -
Especially on November night,
Amongst the wind-whipped pine!

ROBERT J MUMMERY

The Glutton's Fall

Ten years ago my gluttony began,
I tripped up and started to roll.
One more cake and those crisps,
Down, down, down; out of control I go,
Past Mum and Auntie May.
They stared in shock and
Shouted, 'You'll get hurt,'
As I hurried on my way.
'If I could slow down,
Do you not think I would?'
I passed the doctor and he called out
'I advise you – stop!'
It's too difficult to listen,
Too hard to brake.
More chocolate, another sweet, some chips.
Finally my journey's complete.
My rolling meets its final destination
Saint Christopher's Hospital.

Hannah Page

LADIES OF THE SKIES

Do you believe in angels, the ladies of the skies?
For they look down upon us with their tender loving eyes.

They look after your body
They look after your soul
They look after everyone
Until they grow grey and old

They walk by your side
Throughout your young and old lifetime
And try to keep away from you
All of the world's pains and sorrows
Because every loving and caring angel
Now up in Heaven above
Was at one time someone's mother
Down here on Earth below.

DONALD JOHN TYE

The Snowman

The snow fell firm but gently around our little town
In every field and pasture
Rest a snowman could be found
Some say that snowmen don't have souls
They melt and drift away
To reappear on Christmas Eve
And then when temperatures plummet low
Again on Christmas Day
The one I still remember beyond the shaded wood
My childhood of lost Christmasses
In winter chill he stood
He rose above that frozen ground
Six feet of snow and ice, a carrot for his runny nose
And bits of coal for eyes
Robust, a lonely figure, cold winds no force
Could move, just chilling in the shaded wood
Long shadows of the spruce
No person can remember or child of yesteryear
Who built the towering snowman
Upon that hill each year
When spring came round he's melt away
To reappear on Christmas Eve
And then when temperatures plummet low
Again on Christmas Day.

OSCAR

FORWARD POETRY INFORMATION

We hope you have enjoyed reading this book - and that you will continue to enjoy it in the coming years.

If you like reading and writing poetry drop us a line, or give us a call, and we'll send you a free information pack.

Alternatively if you would like to order further copies of this book or any of our other titles, then please give us a call or log onto our website at www.forwardpoetry.co.uk

Forward Poetry Information
Remus House
Coltsfoot Drive
Peterborough
PE2 9BF
(01733) 890099